RAFA NADAL

RAFA NADAL

THE KING OF THE COURT

DOMINIC BLISS

IVY PRESS

Brimming with creative inspiration, how-to projects, and useful information to enrich your everyday life, quarto.com is a favourite destination for those pursuing their interests and passions.

First published in the UK in 2022 by
Ivy Press
An imprint of The Quarto Group
The Old Brewery, 6 Blundell Street
London N7 9BH, United Kingdom
T (0)20 7700 6700
www.Quarto.com

Design by Darren Jordan, Rockjaw Creative

A catalogue record for this book is available from the British Library.

ISBN: 978-0-7112-7613-0
E-book ISBN: 978-0-7112-7615-4

Printed in Bosnia and Herzegovina
10 9 8 7 6 5 4 3 2 1

This book is not endorsed by Rafael Nadal. The author is grateful for the interviews that Rafael Nadal has given him during the course of his remarkable playing career.

CONTENTS

INTRODUCTION

They call him the "raging bull". When you see Rafa charging and sweating round the court, grinding opponents into submission with a combination of power, speed and raw muscle, it's obvious why. The nickname even gave rise to the personal logo you see on his tennis kit and merchandise – two symmetrical bull horns and thunderbolts.

Don't be fooled by all this taurine machismo though. Inside the muscular superhero you see on court is a human being as vulnerable as the rest of us. Every now and then that vulnerability exhibits itself in Rafa's quirky tics and rituals.

That is what makes this man so intriguing: a combination of mere mortal and Herculean demi-god, or Clark Kent and Superman, as he himself once explained it. Sometimes one has the impression that beneath the superhero exoskeleton is a scared little boy peeping out. After all, as you'll discover in these pages, this is a grown man who still sleeps with the light on and is upset by thunderstorms.

This book examines in depth these two aspects of Rafa's persona – the superman and the little boy. It places him firmly in his island home of Mallorca. It questions how he has become defined by other attributes: his left-handedness, his aggressive playing style, his business interests, his Spanishness, his Uncle Toni, his family and friends, his wife Mery, and his insatiable appetite for more and more Grand Slam titles.

Interspersed between these examinations of Rafa's human side are ten of the most important matches of his career so far. Starting with his first major scalp on the ATP tour, back in 2003, we chart the peaks of his career, as he developed into the world-beating force that we all know and love today. Included are his key Grand Slam mileposts, his debut Davis Cup Final and his Olympic gold medal match.

Meanwhile, dotted throughout the book is a series of statistical infographics offering another crucial insight into his on-court career. Sport, especially a sport like tennis, is always a combination of human character and mathematical statistics. To truly understand Rafa the tennis player, both aspects need to be assessed.

RIGHT: Rafa after his win at the Australian Open in 2022.

It's true that I went through some tough situations during all my career. But with the positive attitude and with the right people around – they were a key – I was able to find a way to keep going.

Rafa Nadal

EARLY YEARS

In the old days, Manacor was famous for two things: furniture making and artificial pearls. Since the early noughties, though, both those industries have been totally eclipsed by the constantly growing renown of one famous Mallorcan – arguably the most famous Mallorcan ever to draw breath – Rafa Nadal. Now recognised throughout the world, this tennis player, who (at the time of writing) had 21 Grand Slam singles titles to his name, has placed his home town firmly on the map.

In the grand scheme of things, Manacor is no special town. After the capital, Palma de Mallorca, it's the second or third most important centre on the island, depending on your opinion.

The guidebooks are not especially kind. "Home town of the tennis star Rafael Nadal, industrial Manacor declares its business long before you arrive, with vast roadside hoardings promoting its furniture, wrought-iron and artificial pearl factories," says the *Rough Guide*. "On the strength of these, Manacor has risen to become Mallorca's second city, much smaller than Palma but large enough to have spawned unappetising suburbs on all sides. Locals, however, insist that Manacor is a 'big town, not a city', and in keeping with this, its old centre has been attractively restored, its more important buildings polished and scrubbed, its avenues and piazzas planted with shrubs and trees."

Plain and rather industrial would be a fair way to describe the town, although it does have some prettier buildings. The town website boasts of its school of music and dance, its history museum, its library, its Catalan language institute, its theatre. These are all just sideshows, though, to the town's main act – its most famous son.

Rafa's name is now inextricably linked to the island he was born on and still inhabits. Every Mallorcan, native and ex-pat immigrant alike, knows who he is, what he does, and what he looks like. It wouldn't be unreasonable to dub Rafa "Senor Mallorca".

Rafael Nadal Parera was born on June 3rd 1986. Like all Spaniards, his first family name – the surname that everyone knows him by – is courtesy of his father, Sebastián Nadal, while his second surname derives from his mother, Ana Mariá Parera. Incidentally, in Mallorqui, the Catalan dialect spoken across the island, Nadal means Christmas – from the same root as the English word 'natal', as in the birth of Jesus Christ.

Rafa started playing tennis at the age of four, at his local club, Club Tenis Manacor, on Avenida del Parc (Park Avenue), on the east side of the town centre. Modernised since those early days, the facility now includes five tennis courts, two squash courts and two padel courts – the latter for a popular ball sport played on a smaller walled court. But back in the early 1990s, when Rafa first started hanging out there, you might politely describe it as unassuming. The tacky-looking central clubhouse with a restaurant on the first floor used to serve good pizzas alongside a well-stocked bar. The décor, though, was shabby mid-century, in need of a bit of love.

Despite spawning one of the most famous European tennis players ever to wield a racket, nowadays the club offers surprisingly little evidence that Rafa spent much of his youth here. There are a couple of cheap posters tacked to the walls here and there. But there's no statue of the man; no court named in his honour; no plaque encouraging young Manacorians to follow in their hero's footsteps. The nearby, and much larger, high-tech, more impressive tennis centre that Rafa and his family have since built – the Rafa Nadal Academy and Rafa Nadal Sports Centre – have totally eclipsed the small club he learned his craft in all those years ago.

LEFT: Club Tenis Manacor, where Rafa learned his craft.

At the time, young Rafa and his family lived in an apartment just across the road from the tennis club. His Uncle Toni worked there as a coach. Rafa was already a keen footballer, often seen playing on the streets of Manacor with his friends. One day, he joined in with a group of young tennis players his uncle was coaching. Toni said his nephew initially found the sport boring compared to football. Rafa himself later recalled being a natural player, right from the start. "The first time I played, I already had a good touch," he said. "I already played well."

Until the age of 13, when Toni started coaching him solo, young Rafa used to join in with his uncle's group sessions. His status as nephew by no means guaranteed any special treatment, though. "Toni was tough on me right from the start, tougher than on the other children," Rafa recalled in his 2011 biography *Rafa: My Story*. "He demanded a lot of me, pressured me hard. He'd use rough language, he'd shout a lot, he'd frighten me – especially when the other boys didn't turn up and it was just the two of us. If I saw I'd be alone with him when I arrived for training, I'd get a sinking feeling in my stomach."

BELOW LEFT: Rafa's Uncle Toni, coaching his protégé at Roland Garros in 2006.

BELOW RIGHT: Competing at Les Petits As, Europe's leading junior tournament, in southwest France. Rafa won it in 2000.

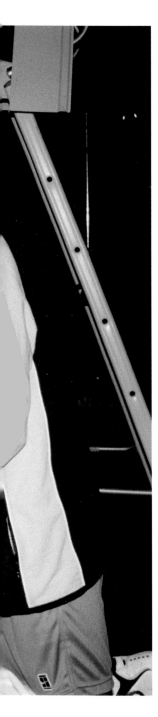

LEFT: Even as a youngster, Rafa was popular with his fans. Here he signs autographs at Les Petits As tournament, in France.

Rafa claims Toni picked on him, even "discriminated against" him, forcing him to collect more balls at the end of the training sessions – many more than the other young players in his charge. Toni would order Rafa to sweep the clay courts after each group session. And he wouldn't hesitate to pelt him with a tennis ball from the other side of the court when his concentration drifted. On several occasions, Rafa went home crying to his mother. The player now believes all that tough love helped to build the resilience and mental strength he later displayed in professional matches.

There was no lack of discipline in Rafa's upbringing. While Toni insisted his nephew behaved impeccably on the court – to this day you'll never see him throw a racket in anger – Rafa's parents drummed into him politeness and decorum in everyday life. They taught him table manners, etiquette and respect for others. When visitors came to the family home Rafa would always be expected to greet them. In the street he was taught to exchange formalities with family acquaintances. When Rafa's youth football team lost matches, his father even went as far as insisting his son approach individual members of the winning team to congratulate them.

The first grandchild in the family, Rafa was always fussed over by his grandparents, uncles and aunts. These include Don Rafael Nadal, his paternal grandfather; Pedro Parera, his maternal grandfather; Marilén Nadal, his aunt and godmother; and Juan Parera, his uncle and godfather. During his youth, all members of Rafa's extended family lived in Manacor or in the neighbouring beach resort of Porto Cristo. Rafa once described his upbringing as "a fairy-tale childhood". Despite the fact his parents are now divorced, he still credits much of his sporting success to this strong, stable family background.

In Spain, sons and daughters will often live with their parents until they get married. When they finally live apart, at weekends they will without fail congregate in a large family group. This is a culture where people regularly stay out late socialising, often beyond midnight. It's not unusual to see adults heading out to restaurants in the evening, with their toddlers or babies sleeping in prams next to them. So, as a youngster, Rafa would join his extended family in bars and restaurants. He also remembers playing football whenever he could with his uncles.

Football loomed large in the Nadal family. Sebastián and Toni's other brothers were both professional players. Uncle Rafael played at a lower level in the Mallorca league, while Uncle Miguel Angel reached the very top of international football. A defender and midfielder for FC Barcelona, Real Mallorca and the Spanish national team, he was nicknamed "The Beast of Barcelona" by the British tabloid newspapers thanks to his physical presence and strength in the air. *The Times* once listed him among the "hardest footballers" of all time. He was dominant in the 1990s, helping Barça win multiple trophies, including the European Cup and five La Liga titles. At international level, he played for Spain 62 times, including at three World Cups.

As a youngster, Rafa would regularly watch his uncle play at Real Mallorca's home ground in Palma, and once, at the age of ten, accompanied him to FC Barça's Camp Nou stadium to join in with the other team players after a training session. All this meant the Nadal family were well accustomed to having a sports superstar in their fold, and it might explain why they seemed so unfazed by Rafa's subsequent success.

"My uncle gave me a glimpse of the life I was to live," Rafa later wrote. "He made money and he became famous; he appeared in the media, and he was mobbed and cheered wherever he went. But he never took himself too seriously."

Rafa's father's career was less glamorous than Miguel Angel's, but ultimately more successful. He is now one of Mallorca's best-known businessmen. (See Chapter 6.) Back when Rafa was a child, he was already running a successful glass-making company, supplying windows, doors and table tops for the booming construction industry that had developed thanks to Mallorca's popularity as a holiday island.

Rafa's mother, too, had experience in business, owning and running a perfume shop in Manacor. She later gave this up to focus on raising Rafa and his little sister, Maribel.

Younger by five years, Maribel has always been incredibly close to her brother. Unusually for siblings of such different ages, brother and sister often used to socialise together, Rafa always quick to invite Maribel on evenings out with his friends. Even now, he claims to miss her when he travels abroad on the ATP tour.

RIGHT: Rafa's sister Maribel, in Palma de Mallorca in 2011.

Just like the other members of the family, Maribel has never allowed her brother's global fame to alter her relationship with him. Even when she moved to Barcelona to study sports education at university, she chose to keep quiet about her famous brother. It was only after a lecturer spotted Maribel in TV footage of one of Rafa's Roland Garros matches that university colleagues outside of her closest circle of friends even discovered who her brother was.

Sport, mostly in the form of football or tennis, occupied the lion's share of Rafa's youth. When he wasn't hitting yellow balls at Club Tenis Manacor, he was kicking large, white ones at the local Manacor football club. A self-confessed football fanatic, he dreamed of becoming a professional player. At the age of 11, playing left wing, he helped his youth team win the Balearic Islands championship, describing the joy he felt at that triumph as equal to the elation he felt years later, winning a tennis Grand Slam title.

Meanwhile, his tennis skills were growing exponentially, nurtured by Toni and his coaching. At this stage Rafa was hitting balls for an hour and a half a day, five days a week. Toni would work him hard, encouraging him to analyse his game endlessly.

By the age of eight, Rafa had won the Under-12s category of the Balearic Islands championship. No mean feat, considering he was up against nine-, ten- and eleven-year-olds in a competition open to children from all four islands of the archipelago – Mallorca, Menorca, Ibiza and Formentera.

While Toni kept pushing Rafa intensely hard on the court, no one pushed him harder than Rafa himself. "Rafa was a very enthusiastic young kid who loved sport," Toni once said. "I have always said I like the passion in things. I do not like to see people who don't have a passion for what they do. This is what Rafa has, ever since he was small. The intention was to realise that potential."

Toni refused to indulge his nephew, however. He strived constantly to keep him humble, even as his tennis blossomed. He taught him the importance of respecting opponents at all times, and of the need to present a calm, serious exterior during matches. Toni admits he would play down, even belittle Rafa's success in those early tournaments. Rather than praise his nephew for the matches he won, it was his style to specify the improvements he needed to make to his game. Any sign of triumph was quickly swept under the carpet.

The other adults in Rafa's family were sceptical of Toni's tough methods. Ultimately, though, they all gave him free rein to carry on applying the pressure.

One incident, in particular, sums up the way Toni would purposefully deflate Rafa's tournament wins. By the time he reached 11 years old, Rafa was playing so expertly that he managed to win the Spanish junior national championships in the Under-12 category. Naturally, he and his family were joyous. But not Toni. While all the others wanted to celebrate, the dour uncle phoned up the Spanish tennis federation, pretending to be a sports reporter, and asked them to provide him with the names of the last 25 junior champions of the title Rafa had just won. He then read out all 25 names, asking his nephew if he'd heard of any of the players. Only a fifth of the 25 had gone on to achieve anything in professional tennis. According to Toni, this proved that Rafa himself had just a one-in-five chance of success on the professional tour.

"I demanded a lot from Rafa because I cared a lot," Toni later said in an interview with the BBC. "I believe in the work and I believe in the players who are strong enough to cope with the intensity of this work. I cannot understand another style of life. This is why I was like this with Rafa. I knew he could cope."

It was a similar attitude a few years later when Rafa won a Nike-sponsored junior tournament in South Africa. On his return to Mallorca, his godmother organised a homecoming party in his grandparents' apartment, decorating the wall with a huge, if slightly tongue-in-cheek, banner of congratulation. But Rafa never made it to the party. Toni intercepted him at the door, pulled the banner off the wall, reprimanded the godmother, and, as a punishment for vanity, forced Rafa to turn up for an early-morning training session the following day.

"I wanted him to know that everything he achieved at that age was not very important in terms of the bigger picture," Toni later said. "I wanted to dampen the expectation. I wanted him to know it was only a little step, and if he wanted to progress he had to continue to work very hard."

BELOW: Rafa's father Sebastián, his wife Mery and his mother Ana Maria watch their boy play in Rome in 2014.

TALLEST PLAYERS
FASTEST SERVERS

How Rafa compares to present and past players.

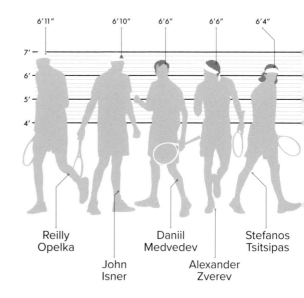

6'11" 6'10" 6'6" 6'6" 6'4"

7'
6'
5'
4'

Reilly
Opelka

John
Isner

Daniil
Medvedev

Alexander
Zverev

Stefanos
Tsitsipas

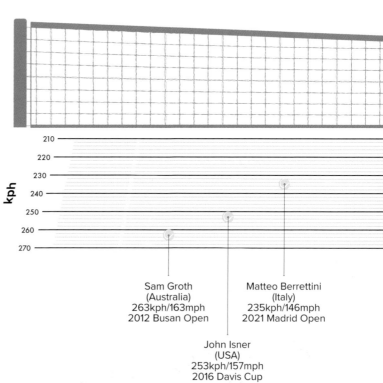

kph

210
220
230
240
250
260
270

Sam Groth
(Australia)
263kph/163mph
2012 Busan Open

John Isner
(USA)
253kph/157mph
2016 Davis Cup

Matteo Berrettini
(Italy)
235kph/146mph
2021 Madrid Open

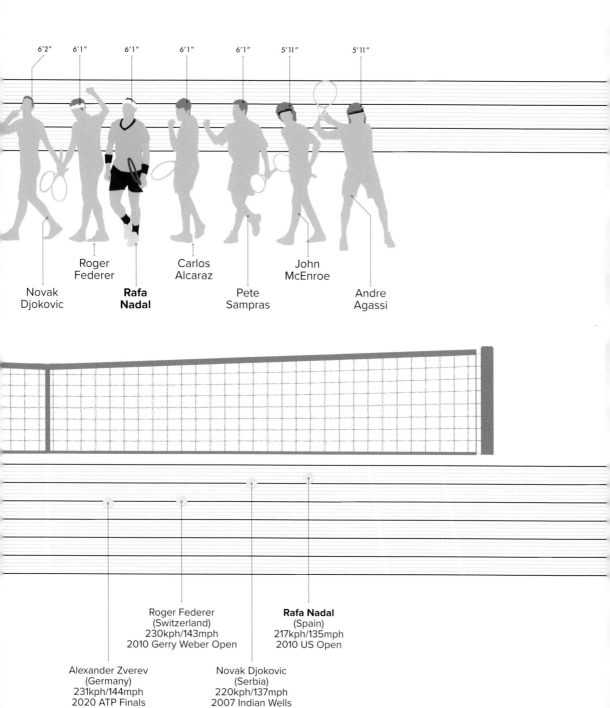

6'2" — Novak Djokovic

6'1" — Roger Federer

6'1" — Rafa Nadal

6'1" — Carlos Alcaraz

6'1" — Pete Sampras

5'11" — John McEnroe

5'11" — Andre Agassi

Alexander Zverev
(Germany)
231kph/144mph
2020 ATP Finals

Roger Federer
(Switzerland)
230kph/143mph
2010 Gerry Weber Open

Novak Djokovic
(Serbia)
220kph/137mph
2007 Indian Wells

Rafa Nadal
(Spain)
217kph/135mph
2010 US Open

Harsh though it was, this tactic certainly worked. Rafa later travelled to Madrid to compete in the Spanish national championships at Under-14 level. During his first-round match he fell over, breaking the little finger on his left hand – his dominant hand. The pain was intense, but Rafa refused to pull out. Nor dared he complain to Toni, knowing there would be no sympathy. Gritting his teeth through every match, eventually he reached the final where he beat his close friend Toméu Salva. By the time it came to the winner's ceremony, the pain in his finger was so bad that he had to ask another player to help him hold the trophy aloft for the photos.

At this period of his life, Rafa was playing both tennis and football. There was the added pressure of school work in between. He knew one of the two sports had to be sacrificed. As much as he adored football – and he was certainly a talented player – that was the one he chose to give up. From then on, football was a sport he only played casually or watched as a spectator, throwing his support behind his adored team Real Madrid CF.

Occasionally Rafa would work with another tennis coach based in Palma called Jofre Porta. Years later Porta was still impressed by the determination of the youngster in his charge. He recalled one occasion, in particular, when that determination really shone. At junior level, tennis matches rarely feature line judges, so players have to call their own balls in or out. During a match, on a crucial point, even though Rafa's shot clearly landed in, his opponent called it out. "He said to me: 'It's incredible! He has stolen the match from me!'" Porta remembers. "I replied sarcastically: 'I thought you were this brave boy who could face up to all problems?' He looked at me really seriously, fought his way back into the match and eventually won. This is the mentality of a champion. I remember thousands of examples like this over the years."

During this period, the Nadal family owned two residences. In Manacor there was the five-storey apartment building close to the city's impressive church, Església de Nostra Senyora dels Dolors (Church of our Lady of Sorrows), with its tall, pointed spire and clock tower. The whole extended family spent much of their time in this apartment building – mother, father, uncles, aunts, cousins and grandparents – all on separate floors but very much living in one another's pockets. Eight miles away, in the far prettier seaside town of Porto Cristo, they owned a second apartment building, again with the family split up between the floors.

It was a set-up that Rafa loved. So much so that when, at the age of 14, he was offered a scholarship to train at a tennis academy in Barcelona, on the Spanish mainland (called the High Performance Centre of Sant Cugat), his parents and

Toni turned down the opportunity, worried he might lack discipline living in a city like Barcelona without their supervision.

"This demonstrates that if it's in you, if you want to work, you can work in any place," Toni later said of the family's decision to keep him in Mallorca. "I don't want to believe that you have to go to America, or other places to be a good athlete. You can do it from your house. In my family, we had two athletes who have been successful. Miguel lived and trained his whole life in Manacor, and Rafa does the same things to continue at this level. The advantage of staying with his family was big for Rafa. It was a plus, both in terms of tranquillity and in terms of organisation."

Nevertheless, a year later they decided to send Rafa away to a sports boarding school in the Mallorcan capital, Palma, called Centre de Tecnificacio Esportiva Illes Balears, or CTEIB. He came home only at weekends.

The facilities were superb: tennis courts, an Olympic-sized swimming pool, athletics track, rugby pitch, basketball, volleyball, physiotherapy and sports medicine – all funded by the taxpayer. But Rafa claims he was miserable there. Homesick, he missed his family terribly, and his cosy life in Manacor. He complained about the busy timetable and hardly shone academically, although he did pass his exams.

Porta, his coach at the school, remembers it slightly differently. "Rafa was a normal student. His level of studying was acceptable and he continued until all the travel no longer allowed him to study. His strongest subject was always physical education."

Rafa eventually talked his parents into taking him out of the school. For a while, on the insistence of his mother who wanted her son to attend university, he followed a distance-learning course. That didn't last long as Rafa lost all his school books, leaving them on the aeroplane on a flight to the Canary Islands. "That was the end of my formal education," he said.

From now on, his entire world revolved around one thing and one thing only: tennis.

"I lost to him during an exhibition match. He was 14 years old, but I took heart by thinking that I had lost to a future Roland Garros champion.

1987 Wimbledon champion Pat Cash

THE MATCH

MONTE-CARLO MASTERS
April 16th 2003
Monte-Carlo Country Club, Roquebrune-Cap-Martin, France
2nd Round: Rafa Nadal vs. Albert Costa
Rafa Nadal beat Albert Costa 7–5, 6–3

It was in 2001 that Rafa made his debut on the ATP tour, although his initial forays were at the lower levels of ITF Futures and ATP Challenger tournaments. His first match to earn him ATP rankings points was an ITF Futures tournament in Madrid in September of that year, which he lost to fellow Spaniard Guillermo Platel.

In 2002 he made his debut on the ATP main tour, playing at a clay-court tournament in Mallorca, an event that no longer exists. (There is now a grass-court event called the Mallorca Championships in June, but this is very different.) In the first round he beat Paraguay's Ramon Delgado – his first scalp on the ATP tour proper. For the remainder of that season he ticked off multiple Futures and Challengers, winning minor titles in Alicante, Vigo, Barcelona and Gran Canaria.

It was all invaluable experience in the run-up to his first big-boy match in April 2003. At the tender age of 16, with a world ranking of 109, he was very much thrown in at the deep end as he made his debut at the Monte-Carlo Masters, an ATP Masters tournament at the level just below Grand Slams. And what a debut. In the first round he annihilated Slovakian player Karol Kucera 6–1, 6–2. The second round saw him up against the reigning French Open champion, and certainly one of the best clay-courters on the planet at that time, fellow Spaniard Albert Costa.

Rafa had been in impressive form so far that year, reaching four finals in ATP Challenger events (the level below the main ATP tour), and winning one of them. This was only his fourth match on the main ATP tour. The whole tennis world was excited at the prospect of a new young force on clay. But they hardly expected him to beat Costa. After all, the very experienced 27-year-old (who looked older) had won Roland Garros the year before, and already had a further 11 ATP titles on clay to his name.

Commentating on the match that day for the Fox Sports TV channel were John Barrett and Jason Goodall, two British experts in the sport. "A young man of

RIGHT: In 2003, aged 16, Rafa knew just how important his first win on the Monte Carlo clay would be.

immense promise," said the former, as Rafa walked on court. Crucial to his success, Barrett explained, was the fact that seasoned Spanish player Carlos Moya, another Mallorcan, had been advising him. "He is a mentor to the young man. It's great for somebody as young as this to have somebody as experienced as Moya in his corner."

Goodall agreed: "When you can get that advice from somebody who has been there, done that – a former world number two, a Grand Slam champion – then it's absolutely priceless," he added. "Hopefully that will fast-track this young man to the very top of the game."

Wearing dark shorts, a white shirt and the white headband that would soon become recognised as his trademark, Rafa took a while to get into his stride. Using deft dropshots, and frustrating his older opponent by stretching out the rallies through some courageous defensive play, he began to get the upper hand. As the first set progressed, Costa started playing more and more nervously. The errors began to creep in. Indeed, it was a forehand error that finally handed the first set to Rafa.

3–1 up in the second set, the younger man ramped up the pressure. At deuce, he was pushing Costa deeper behind the baseline with every groundstroke of the rally, ending the point with a net approach and a brilliant, unreturnable smash. He won the next point to stretch 4–1 ahead.

Eventually, exactly two hours after the match had begun, Rafa found himself 5–3 up with a triple match point. But he needed only one of them. Costa fluffed his return, losing 7–5, 6–3.

"I played, indeed, a very good match," Rafa said afterwards. "In the beginning it was a bit average. I think I felt too much respect or was a bit afraid of him. But, during the match, I started to play better and better. I thought maybe [Costa] was scared a little bit because he was playing against a younger player. But, to tell the truth, I was not very confident that I was going to win."

The commentator John Barrett was far more effusive. "A sensational victory for a young man who has announced himself on the world stage in no uncertain fashion, beating arguably the finest clay-court player at the moment."

RIGHT: Rafa and Carlos Moya – his friend, mentor and fellow Mallorcan – at a sponsor's event in Barcelona.

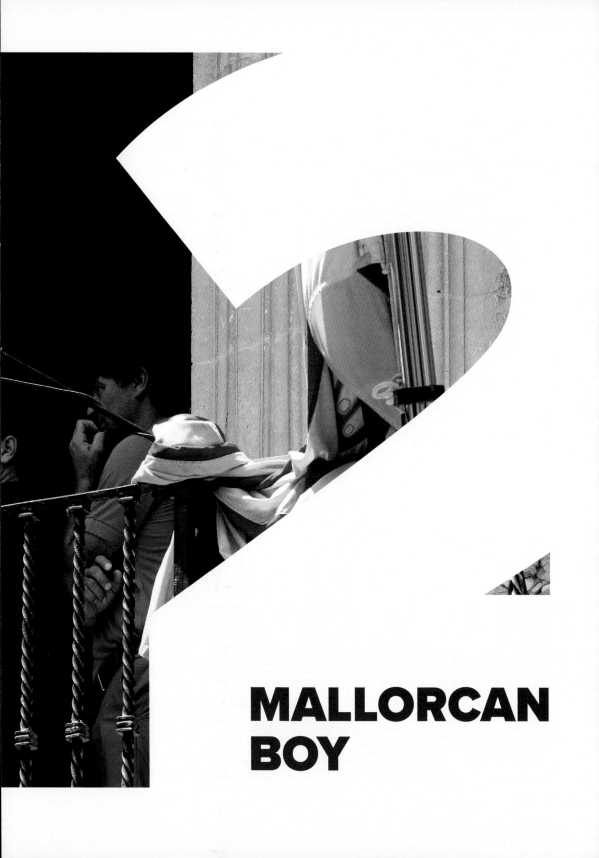

MALLORCAN
BOY

According to family folklore, there have been Nadals living on Mallorca since the 14th century, back when it was known as Regnum Maioricae, or the Kingdom of Mallorca. While Rafa himself has occupied the island for a mere 35 years, to understand the man and his place in Mallorcan society, it's important to get a grasp of Balearic history.

The island's key position in the Mediterranean means that, over the centuries, it has been invaded on a regular basis. First by the Talayotic people (probably from Asia Minor), and later by the Phoenicians, the Greeks, the Carthaginians, the Romans, the Vandals, the Byzantines, and various North African powers – all of whom took their turn at pillaging and subjugating.

By the Middle Ages Mallorca had started to prosper, even enjoying periods of independence, before finally becoming part of unified Spain in the early 18th century.

After the Spanish Civil War (1936–1939), from which the islanders emerged relatively unscathed, the economy was turned completely on its head. Mass package tourism arrived with all the subtlety of a Club 18–30 party night. Palma de Mallorca international airport opened in the late 1950s and was soon handling a million passengers a year. Before the global pandemic struck in 2020, this figure had increased to nearly 30 million a year, with tourism responsible for 80 per cent of the islanders' GDP.

But in recent years, the direction of that tourism has changed radically. The island's government has realised that cheap package tours don't represent much of a future for their Mediterranean outpost. They would rather welcome fewer visitors, but ones with more money in their pockets. This has led to restrictions on mass-market coastal developments

LEFT: Rafa enlists the help of Roger Federer at the opening of his tennis academy in Manacor in October 2016.

and the promotion of more sustainable rural tourism. Now Mallorcans are offering sports and activity holidays, and boutique agritourism accommodation (or 'agroturismos') to more upmarket visitors tired of mass-market beach holidays. The success of Rafa's tennis academy, which attracts players from all over Europe, is linked to this.

Rafa himself remains fairly pragmatic when asked about the impact of tourism on his beloved island. "I think it is good for the economy and it is good for the locals. I think Mallorca is the best place on Earth and that's the reason why they come, I suppose."

Meanwhile there has been a resurgence in Balearic regional pride. While it is far less strident than the Catalonian independence movements on the mainland, nonetheless, Mallorcans are starting to celebrate their culture; to distinguish themselves from the overbearing influence of Castilian Spain.

Nowhere is this more evident than in their language. While all Mallorcans are completely fluent in Castilian Spanish, it's not their everyday tongue. Rafa and his fellow islanders speak a Catalan dialect called Mallorqui, a language almost as different from Castilian Spanish as English is from Dutch. So *buenos dias* is *bon dia*; *adios* is *adéu*; *muchas gracias* is *moltes gracis*. To truly understand the workings of Rafa's brain, one must realise that Mallorqui is the lingua franca he operates in day to day when he's back home with his family and friends. Mallorqui is the language he chats in, thinks in, dreams in.

But, for someone as famous as Rafa, there is a fine line to tread between Mallorcan regional pride and Spanish patriotism. Prudently, he never downplays his Spanishness. Yes, he won't miss the chance to declare his adoration of Mallorca, but he is quick to remind everyone that he is also Spanish.

Spain is a fragile federation of fiercely proud regions, many like Mallorca, with their own language or dialect. Most of Rafa's sponsors are Castilian Spanish rather than Mallorcan, and are headquartered on the mainland. By accentuating his Mallorcan identity too much, he would risk alienating them. The financial cost would be enormous to him.

Nowadays, the tennis player is something of a de facto ambassador for his island. In December 2014 he was officially named as the "Favourite Son of Mallorca" at a special ceremony. It turns out, of the 11 islanders who have ever received the award, he was the only living recipient.

Given his international appeal and fame, you could argue that Rafa is the most famous Mallorcan of all time. After all, who else is there?

RIGHT: Rafa greets fans at Manacor's town hall after returning home from his 2008 Wimbledon victory.

BELOW: Nadal serves the ball during his exhibition match against Rainer Schuttler in July 2005.

There was the poet Miquel Costa i Llobera, the singers Concha Buika, Joan Miquel Oliver and Maria del Mar Bonet, music producer DJ Sammy, painter Miquel Barceló, filmmaker Agustí Villaronga, and plenty of other sportsmen, including footballers Miguel Angel Nadal (Rafa's uncle), Marco Asensio and Xisco Muñoz, motorcyclists Joan Mir and Jorge Lorenzo, and tennis player Carlos Moya (Rafa's current coach). But few of these have become renowned outside of Spain, tennis or MotoGP, and none has earned global fame like Rafa.

While the Nadal family still owns the large apartment building in Manacor, nowadays, Rafa spends most of his time with his wife María Francisca (or Mery, as he calls her) at their seaside villa in Porto Cristo, the fishing town east of Manacor. (Its value has been estimated at US$4.3 million.) Here the family owns a string of villas – three at the last count, but possibly more by the time you read this. Even more than in Manacor, Rafa feels safe at his Porto Cristo home, and can often be seen playing football on the local beach with friends. Fortunately none of the locals bother him for selfies. Should he ever receive hassle for his celebrity status, it will be from a tourist rather than a Mallorcan. In any case, he owns a 24-metre yacht, often moored in the harbour at Porto Cristo, which he can escape to if he needs privacy.

In 2020 Rafa took delivery of this vessel, a customised Sunreef 80 Power catamaran, which he has christened *Great White*. It was on a visit to Cannes Boat Show that his head was first turned by the leisure yacht. It features a main-deck saloon, a front terrace, four guest cabins and Rafa's own suite with a fold-out balcony. There's also a flying bridge, a wet bar, a barbecue, and a garage for jet skis. Most of the time Rafa and Mery sail within the Balearics archipelago. "The boat, for me, is like my house," Rafa says. "I can go out and enjoy, and at the same time disconnect a little bit from everything."

Rafa also owns a mansion home in the Caribbean nation the Dominican Republic. It's reported he was gifted the property in return for promoting the complex it sits in, in the tourist city of La Romana.

Although he admits that fast cars scare him to death (see Chapter 5), they do play a part in his life. Occasionally you'll spot him behind the wheel – always driving very cautiously – on the roads of eastern Mallorca. One of his more lucrative sponsorship contracts means he often has a new Kia at his disposal. The latest delivery was a Kia EV6 electric car. He also owns, or has owned at one time, an Aston Martin DBS, a Ferrari 458 Italia, a convertible Mercedes SL 55 AMG and a Mercedes AMG GT S.

ABOVE: Celebrated as 'Favourite Son of Mallorca', in 2014, Rafa unveils a painting in his honour.

RIGHT: Sharing an award ceremony with Mallorcan MotoGP champion Jorge Lorenzo in 2010.

Relaxation time away from tennis is important for Rafa's psychological state of mind. Lorenzo Cazzaniga is a veteran tennis reporter who knows the player perhaps better than any other journalist outside of Mallorca. "When he's not playing tennis or training, he does just three things," Cazzaniga explains. "He goes fishing, or he hangs out at the beach with his friends, or he plays golf. He is a golf fanatic, and a very good player. I've been told that, nowadays, he gets more upset at losing at golf than at tennis."

Cazzaniga says Rafa has no interest in the celebrity lifestyle that certain other tennis players pursue. He may occasionally go out late to bars in Manacor or Porto Cristo with his friends ("I barely touch alcohol, but I do go out dancing and sometimes stay up till six in the morning," he explained in his autobiography), but he is rarely seen at VIP events.

"He doesn't want any changes in his life," Cazzaniga explains. "He's a very routine guy. He wants to stay with his wife, his family, the same old friends. He still hangs out with his childhood friends. And when he finishes his tennis career, he will probably lead a very – I don't want to say boring lifestyle – but a very basic lifestyle. Albeit with millions of dollars in the bank. He's not the type of person who's going to move to Miami or New York or Dubai." Even when Rafa and Mery take their holidays, they rarely leave the Balearics.

The importance of Rafa's relationship with his childhood friends should not be underestimated. While many successful celebrities naturally lose touch with friends from their youth, he never has. That's down to a combination of loyalty, humility and the simple fact that he always returns to Mallorca in between tournaments.

"We are normal people, attached to family traditions and values," he once explained. "I go to the supermarket and to the cinema. When I come home, I take up the same life as before. For me, real life, my normal life, it's not tournament life. I have kept my childhood friends, I play football with my cousins. I find it's crucial to be able to return home after spending months travelling around the world and settling back into my old life. It's fundamental."

Among his closest compadres are Toméu Artigues, Toméu Salva, Miguel Angel Munar and Joan Suasi. Although Rafa is now married to Mery, with all the responsibilities that marriage brings, he can still often be seen playing beach football with his friends, entertaining them on his yacht, going on fishing trips, or hanging out with them at bars and nightclubs in Porto Cristo and Manacor.

One of his favourite haunts is the Nadal family-owned restaurant called Sa Punta, in the coastal town of Cala Bona, a few miles north of Porto Cristo. Here, the head chef Andrés Moreno offers classic Spanish dishes such as Iberico ham, Spanish omelette and gazpacho soup, as well as fish and seafood dishes like bluefin tuna, sea bass, octopus and lobster. "The combination of the ocean view, the service, and the food – I always order the catch of the day, grilled – make it a perfect spot," Rafa says, with his marketing hat on.

It's golf, though, that enthuses Rafa the most. More than anything, he loves to spend his spare hours on the smarter golf courses of Mallorca. A particular favourite is Pula Golf, a few miles northeast of Manacor. It's at this course that, in 2013, he joined forces with top Spanish professional golfer José María Olazábal to set up an annual charity tournament called the Olazábal & Nadal Invitational.

While travelling and competing on the ATP tour, Rafa's spare time is much more limited. Like that of most professional players, his is a whirlwind existence, lived at a thousand miles an hour, between airports, hotels and tournament venues, with just the odd snatched moment of rest and relaxation in between. He likes to go out for dinner with whichever members of his support team happen to be on tour with him. "We are always trying to go out for dinner," he said in a recent GQ interview. "To forget, to distract yourself a little bit [from] all the routines."

Music is another distraction, played through his precious Apple Airpods. "When you are on the plane, or before matches, I use music," he says. "I like almost everything. I can listen to opera, classical music, pop, rock. It depends on the moment and the mood. Electronic music is the only music I can't [listen to]."

The minute a tournament is over, however, this homeboy is desperate to fly back to his island home. "I appreciate being a Mallorcan," he once said. "The first thing that I do when I'm playing in other countries, whether I win or lose in the tournament, is to seek the fastest way to go back to Mallorca."

AGE WHEN WINNING FIRST GRAND SLAM

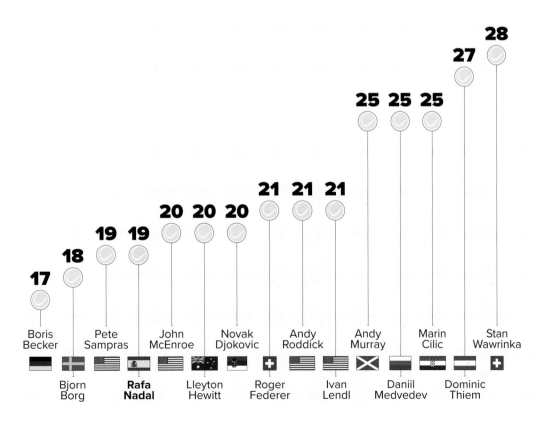

TOP LEFT: Rafa with Mallorcan friends in 2011.

BOTTOM LEFT: With his future wife Mery in 2010.

OPPOSITE TOP RIGHT: Competing in a golf tournament in 2020.

OPPOSITE TOP LEFT: Rafa and his childhood friend Tomeu Salva.

OPPOSITE BOTTOM: In the kitchen with golfer José Maria Olazabal.

If he couldn't return to his island whenever he wanted to, after playing tournaments, I think he would go mad.

Ana María Parera,
Rafa's Mother

THE MATCH

IDEA PROKOM OPEN
August 15th 2004
Sopocki Klub Tenisowy, Sopot, Poland
Final: Rafa Nadal vs. José Acasuso
Rafa Nadal beat José Acasuso 6–3, 6–4

The year he turned 18, 2004, was a difficult one for Rafa. Criss-crossing the globe, by mid-April he had already competed in India, New Zealand, Australia – where he had reached the third round of the Australian Open, losing to Leyton Hewitt – Czech Republic, Italy, Dubai, California, Florida and Portugal. All of which took a massive toll on his body so that, by the time the clay-court season had started, he found himself in severe pain, suffering with a stress fracture in his left ankle. That spring and early summer, frustrated, he was forced to sit out most of the tournaments on his favourite surface, including Roland Garros. So, as soon as the fracture had repaired itself, he was keen to get back on the red stuff; and desperate to secure his first title on the ATP tour.

In August he travelled to Poland to compete in the Idea Prokom Open, staged at the Sopocki Klub Tenisowy, a clay-court venue overlooking the beaches along the Baltic coast, not far north of Gdansk.

Well rested after his forced break, the sixth seed was in fine form, winning every set he played that week. Moreover, it was a wise choice of comeback tournament after his injury. Held after the end of Europe's clay-court season, when most of the world's elite were on the North American hard-court swing, it had failed to attract many dangerous players. Indeed, with Rafa ranked at 71 in the world, all his opponents in Sopot were below him in the ATP rankings.

In the final, he found himself up against Argentinean player José Acasuso, another clay-court specialist. The first set started off unremarkably, its most watchable point coming at two games all, 15–all, with Rafa serving. The rally then played out over the course of 19 shots. During this, Rafa successfully had his opponent running up and down his baseline, from one side to the other, like a puppet on a string. The latter returned everything that was thrown at him, but couldn't dictate Rafa's movements in the same way. Serving for the set at 5–3 up, Rafa easily wrapped up the final game, thanks to some unforced errors from his opponent.

For most, this was their first chance to see the Mallorcan shining in an ATP final.
He had reached, and lost, the final at the Auckland tournament in January, but that
was in New Zealand, the other side of the planet.

In the first game of the second set, with Acasuso serving, Rafa looked to be in
control again, suddenly handed three break points at 0–40. Initially the
Argentinean clawed his way back to deuce but eventually handed Rafa the break
of serve.

Play continued with serve until 4–2, after which Rafa broke again to go 5–2
up. He was now serving for the match.

While his court coverage remained fast and furious, his serves started to become tentative, the pressure of victory no doubt weighing on his mind. Acasuso realised he now had to take chances if he wanted to turn this match around. He started hitting his groundstrokes much flatter, firing some fast, pinpoint, down-the-line shots that flustered his opponent. He even followed up those shots to kill the rally off at the net. On the first deuce, he pushed Rafa further and further back with each shot until the Spaniard was almost bouncing off the back netting. Finally, Acasuso broke serve. Was the Mallorcan going to blow it?

In the next game, Rafa defended brilliantly, returning shots that other men would have abandoned. At 30–all, he pushed Acasuso wide on his forehand, forcing him to snatch a return that fell into the net for an unforced error. This gave Rafa his first match point. The Spaniard chose to mark it by jumping in the air and giving a double fist pump. Nowadays he's unlikely to celebrate an opponent's unforced error in that manner. But it showed just how hungry he was for his first ATP title.

There was still work to do, however. Acasuso's first serve was called a let. The Argentinean, under intense pressure, couldn't believe the ball had clipped the net. Begging for a re-appraisal, he approached the chair, and placed his hand on the umpire's knee. The latter smiled but wouldn't be swayed.

Perhaps this was the distraction he needed to disturb his opponent's concentration. The second serve was strong, and Rafa failed to return it. It required several more hard-fought points, and a dispute over a service call, but Acasuso managed to hold serve to take the score to 5–4, with Rafa still leading.

The Mallorcan was in no mood to string out proceedings any longer. He quickly wrapped up the final game, jumping up and down with his arms in the air as he secured his precious maiden ATP title, winning 6–3, 6–4.

"I was very calm out there today," he said afterwards. "My goal at the start of the year was a top 20 spot, but I was injured for three months and am now aiming for the top 25 to 40 by the year end."

The Sopot win actually placed him just inside the world top 50, a position he maintained for the rest of the season, as he reached the second round of both the US Open and the ATP Masters in Madrid.

OPPOSITE: Playing in New Zealand in 2004.

LEFT-HANDED

Adisproportionate number of tennis's elite are left-handed: John McEnroe, Martina Navratilova, Jimmy Connors, Rod Laver, Goran Ivanisevic, Monica Seles, Thomas Muster, Jaroslav Drobny, Guillermo Vilas, Marcelo Rios and, of course, Rafa Nadal.

In the doubles game, too, some of the greatest teams of all time have been lefty/righty pairings: the Bryan brothers, the Woodies (Mark Woodforde and Todd Woodbridge), Rod Laver and Roy Emerson, Tony Roche and John Newcombe, John McEnroe and Peter Fleming, Martina Navratilova and Pam Shriver.

So why do so many champions wield their rackets on the left wing? Is there something about the game of tennis that hands them an advantage? It turns out there is, and it's all down to the simple fact that left-handers are rarer. While lefties are accustomed to playing against righties (since most players are righties), righties are not so used to playing against lefties (since fewer players are lefties). This rarity has benefitted Rafa (and his left-handed colleagues) brilliantly throughout his career.

Chris McManus is a professor of educational psychology at University College London, and author of *Right Hand, Left Hand*. "The left-hander knows far more about their opponent's foibles than does the right-hander, which gives them a competitive edge," he explains.

In 2009, Norbert Hagemann, a sports scientist from the University of Munster in Germany, carried out an intriguing test on tennis players in order to measure the way they anticipated shots from an opponent. He brought together a test sample of 54 right-handed players and 54 left-handed players, all of varying skill levels, from complete novice to

LEFT: Rafa plays tennis left-handed and football left-footed, but writes, brushes his teeth, catches a ball and plays golf with his right hand.

expert. He then required them to watch video clips of right-handed and left-handed expert players before predicting the direction in which their shots would travel back over the net. His volunteers found it more difficult to predict the stroke direction of the left-handed players than of the right-handed players. Both left-handers and right-handers were better at predicting the direction of right-handed strokes.

Hagemann highlighted a theory known among academics as the strategic advantage hypothesis. "Because players become used to the hitting patterns or playing style of right-handed opponents, attacks from the opposite side take them by surprise," he wrote. "In addition to this surprise effect, the motor responses to such an attack may also be under-practised. Because this type of attack by left-handers is less frequent, defensive reactions are less automatic and, therefore, possibly less effective."

It's a similar story in other sports where athletes also strike from one side of the body, facing their opponent: all the racket sports, for example, as well as cricket, boxing, fencing, baseball, softball, volleyball. Since lefties are rarer, they make for trickier opponents.

But tennis does have one other factor that helps out the left-handed players, and that's all down to the geometry of the court. Most of the crucial points during a tennis match – game points or break points – occur when the server is playing to the advantage side (the right-hand side as he faces the court) of the court. If the server is left-handed and the returner is right-handed, the former can swing his serve wide to the right-hander's backhand side, which for most players is the weaker side. This means that on the crunch points, lefties are able to use their biggest weapon against their opponent's weaker arm. (Just look how Rafa has consistently battered Federer's backhand in this manner, to lethal effect.)

Conversely, right-handed servers playing left-handed returners don't have the same advantage on crunch points since a wide serve would end up arriving to their opponent's forehand – generally their stronger stroke. (So when it's Federer's turn to serve, he isn't able to return the insult back across the net to Rafa.)

Greg Rusedski, the British player who reached a ranking of number four in the world, summed it up nicely in an interview with the BBC. "The left-handed serve naturally spins differently when you strike it, which makes it lethal coming from the left side of the court," he explained. "Creating this kind of spin – making the ball swerve and bounce – pushes the ball far out wide, onto a righty's backhand. If my opponent is good enough to get the ball back, the court's wide open for me to take the point."

It's possible there's an added X-factor that benefits left-handed tennis players. And it may have something to do with the way their brains are wired differently compared to most people's. Former American player Mary Carillo, a left-hander herself, analysed this in an interview with *Sports Illustrated* magazine. "Mainly, we're nuts," she said. "You look at all the left-handers in tennis and you've got some real wing nuts: Connors, McEnroe, Goran Ivanisevic, Guillermo Vilas."

She lumps Rafa into this group of crazy players, too. "That kid has a different spin on how to construct points; develop a rally," she added. "He thinks outside the box."

It turns out Rafa's left-handedness is a little more complicated than everyone else's, though. When he first started playing, at the age of four, barely able to see over the net, he used a double-handed grip on both hands, so as to give him the power he needed to send the ball back. One day Uncle Toni informed him how few professional players used two hands on both the forehand and the backhand, and that he needed to switch to using a single-handed forehand. Rafa did what he was told, finding his left hand the most natural.

OUT IN LEFT FIELD

The Grand Slam results of left-handers in the Open Era.

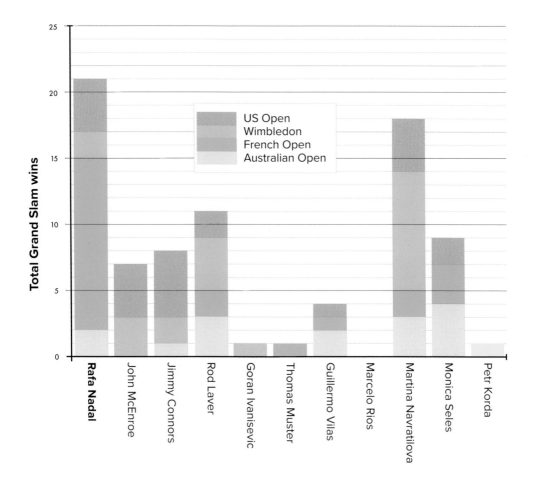

Total Grand Slam wins

Legend:
- US Open
- Wimbledon
- French Open
- Australian Open

Players: Rafa Nadal, John McEnroe, Jimmy Connors, Rod Laver, Goran Ivanisevic, Thomas Muster, Guillermo Vilas, Marcelo Rios, Martina Navratilova, Monica Seles, Petr Korda

LEFTIE NOTES:
- Thomas Muster won the French Open on clay but couldn't get beyond the first round at Wimbledon.
- Chilean tennis player Marcelo Rios was ATP World No.1 in 1988 but never won a Grand Slam tournament.
- Two of the most successful female lefties of the modern era are Martina Navratilova and Monica Seles, with 18 and 9 Grand Slam titles respectively.

"I simply advised him to use his strongest hand," Toni once explained. "That's it."

In an interview with Nike, Toni went into more depth. "It's a strange thing because the only thing he does with his left hand is play tennis. If he has to catch a ball, he always catches it with his right hand. He is right-handed. If he has to throw it, it is always with his right hand. When he was little, he always played with two hands because he didn't have the strength. I thought it was much better to play with one hand than with two because there are hardly any players on the professional circuit who play with two hands. In the end we decided to play with the left. The first tournament he played with his left hand, it was pretty difficult. But hey, it was a step he needed to take."

There's a further complication to his mixed-handedness – and that's the relationship between his dominant hand and his dominant eye. This is explained very well in a book by Argentinean journalist Sebastian Fest, called *Roger Federer & Rafael Nadal: The Lives and Careers of Two Tennis Legends*. Fest discusses Rafa's versatility with an expert in the field called Paul Dorochenko, who explains how some players have their dominant eye and hand on the same side of the body (in which case, they're classified as homogenous), while others have them on opposite sides of their body (classified as crossed). Dorochenko reveals that Rafa is crossed, since his dominant hand is on the left, while his dominant eye is on the right.

"Crossed individuals tend to be poorly disciplined, inconsistent and exhibitionist, but also more creative, intuitive and better at making decisions," Dorochenko tells Fest, claiming that 70 per cent of players in the top 100 world rankings are crossed. "On the other hand, homogenous players are hard-working, ordered, analytical and cerebral, but pressure takes a greater toll on them and affects them negatively when it comes to decision-making."

Although it's hard to accept that Rafa might be poorly disciplined and inconsistent, you could certainly argue his aggressive playing style might stem from some sort of exhibitionism. And he's definitely creative, intuitive and good at making decisions.

There's no doubting that switching from double-handed to left-handed was a fortuitous move for Rafa. Nowadays, just watch how right-handed players struggle to return his serve when it's fired to the advantage side of the court. Given loads of slice, the ball swings really wide, forcing the returner well beyond the tramlines. Even if the returner manages to scramble back a return, he still finds himself totally out of position for the next shot.

All of which begs an obvious question. "Would Rafa be as strong now if he used his right hand?" Toni once mused in an interview with *Tennis* magazine. "That's something we don't know and we will never know."

RIGHT: Rafa plays tennis left-handed but writes right-handed.

THE MATCH

DAVIS CUP FINAL

December 3rd 2004

Estadio Olimpico, Seville, Spain

Match 2: Rafa Nadal vs. Andy Roddick

Rafa Nadal beat Andy Roddick 6–7, 6–2, 7–6, 6–2

In every tennis player's career, there is one pivotal match which signals transition from junior to fully fledged adult. For Rafa, it was his win over Andy Roddick in the second match of the Davis Cup Final between Spain and the US in 2004.

Davis Cup Finals are the highlight of international men's team tennis; the equivalent of the World Cup in football. But unlike the World Cup, the Davis Cup is played every year.

Nowadays, the top level, known as the Davis Cup Finals, sees 18 teams compete at three venues (normally in late November or early December), with round-robin matches, followed by quarter-finals, semi-finals and a final. In previous years, the format was different: 16 teams would play knock-out ties (best of five matches) throughout the season, culminating in the strongest two teams thrashing out the final, usually in December. The five matches of this final, played over the course of a long weekend, consisted of four singles matches and one doubles.

In 2004 it was USA and Spain who proved the strongest, with the latter allowed to choose the venue for the final. Knowing this would be one of the most popular sports events of the year, but also that a clay surface would give them an advantage, the Spanish opted to stage the final at the Estadio Olimpico – or La Cartuja, as it is known to locals – in the southern city of Seville. With a capacity of 60,000 seats, it normally hosts football matches, especially Spain's national team, and features an athletics track surrounding the grass pitch. Since a tennis court would have been lost in the centre, the organisers decided to place the clay court at one end, with a temporary roof erected above. Even sliced in half, there was room for 27,200 spectators, some of whom had camped out in the rain to snap up the last tickets in the days leading up to the tie.

But no one expected to be cheering on the baby of the squad – 18-year-old Rafa. Originally he had been slated to play as one half of the doubles team. Teamed up with Tommy Robredo, the duo would have been cannon fodder, forced to take on the Bryan brothers – at that time the greatest doubles players on the planet. But, bizarrely, at the last minute, team captain Jordi Arrese chose Rafa to play in the second singles match, against USA's imposing weapon: world number two and former US Open champion Andy Roddick.

No one was more shocked than Rafa himself. He considered himself "the kid in the team", more of a cheerleader for his teammates than a serious contender on the court. He remembers being unbelievably excited at the prospect of representing Spain. This was the Davis Cup Final after all, the most important team event in the entire sport.

But there was a problem. After Carlos Moya had won the first singles match, logically the captain ought to have chosen one of Rafa's far more experienced teammates – either Juan Carlos Ferrero or Tommy Robredo – to play the second singles. Rafa was by far the lowest ranked of all four teammates, and had missed more than two months of the season with a stress fracture in his left foot. He remembers considering himself the David to Roddick's Goliath. No surprise, then, that he felt guilty, uncomfortable and apologetic, especially since he had been promoted above his older and wiser compatriots.

Nonetheless, the desire to compete and desperation not to disappoint his teammates meant he embarked on his daunting task with relentless, unstoppable enthusiasm.

That Friday in early December was cool and rainy, in a city where clay tennis is usually viewed in the warm springtime or the searing summer heat. As a result, many in the crowd were sporting pullovers and overcoats. Down on the court, at times it was chilly enough to see the players' breath as they recovered in between points.

Forced to thrash out lengthy rallies on the slow clay, however, both players quickly warmed up.

The first set went to a tiebreak that Rafa soon led 5–2. And then anxiety struck. Roddick fought back to win the tiebreak and the set.

This is when the home advantage really became apparent. Constantly urged on by his fellow Spaniards, Rafa tore his way through the second set, securing it 6–2. Although the American tried desperately to break his opponent's rhythm by charging the net time and time again, it proved an unwise policy. On a surface as slow as that damp, winter clay, Rafa was often afforded the time he needed to cue up for passing shots, even against such a formidable net man as Roddick.

The key to the match was the third set, where both players held set points. Roddick clawed back two on his serve at 5–6, while Rafa saved his one in the

LEFT: In action against Andy Roddick in the 2004 Davis Cup Final in Seville.

BELOW LEFT AND RIGHT: Victory over world number two Andy Roddick surprised everyone.

BOTTOM: Celebrating victory with Carlos Moya.

tiebreak, with a crafty dropshot that his opponent sprinted for but could only dump into the net. The next two points went the Spaniard's way, handing him the set.

Even by Davis Cup standards, the atmosphere in Seville that day was raucous. With over 27,000 clamorous spectators in attendance, cheering every point Rafa won and every point Roddick lost (even the unforced errors), this was, at the time, the largest crowd that had ever attended an official tennis match. (There had been 3,000 more at the Houston Astrodome in 1973 when Billie Jean King beat Bobby Riggs in the Battle of the Sexes, but that had been an exhibition match.) Later, Rafa said he'd tried his utmost to draw energy from these shamelessly partisan supporters. Virtually every winning point was punctuated by pumps of the fist, often directed at his opponent. On the crucial points, those fist pumps went multiple, accompanied by leaps in the air, scissor kicks and howls of delight. Later, once the match was complete, Rafa admitted he'd been foolish to jump so much in celebration, and that all that extra movement had caused more than a little cramping in his legs. All the same, you could tell he was loving every minute of this, his glorious rite of passage.

By the fourth set, Roddick was withering under the assault, both from his opponent and the noisy spectators. At 5–2 in the fourth set, Rafa finally found himself serving for the match. He delivered to Roddick's backhand – nothing fast, nothing tricky. Then it was just a four-shot rally to secure the match, ending in Roddick sending a nervous backhand long.

Immediately Rafa slipped backwards to lie down in celebration, his arms and legs stretched out into a star formation, his bandana falling to the clay. The crowd all round the court erupted with joy. "The noise in my ears felt like a jumbo jet flying low overhead," Nadal later recalled. "50 per cent of the victory was thanks to the audience."

Rafa had fought for three hours and 45 minutes – the longest match he had so far contested during his short career. "In each period of my life, there can be key matches," he said. "This has certainly been the match of my life." Spain went on to win the match 3–2.

One journalist there that day was Christopher Clarey, for the *New York Times*. He described Rafa's performance as "transcendent". "Seldom in the long history of the game have so many spectacular shots been hit from such extreme angles," he wrote. "And though Roddick played beautifully and bravely at times – pushing forward much more than was predictable or prudent on such a slow surface and hitting some remarkable volleys – Nadal's positive energy, passing shots and baseline brio eventually wore him down."

BELOW: Rafa with Carlos Moya.

"For me, the Davis Cup victory over Andy Roddick, that's really the moment when Rafael Nadal became a champion, when he wrote the start of his story, when the public first started to know him.

Carlos Moya

CLAY-COURT TENNIS

▐▐ Clay teaches you how to suffer." So said the legendary Spanish coach José Higueras, who during his career advised the likes of Jim Courier, Roger Federer, Pete Sampras, Sergi Bruguera and Carlos Moya on how to excel on the red stuff. Nor was he exaggerating. With its longer rallies, wider angles and greater physical demands, clay-court tennis has always tested players to the very limit.

It also makes for a wonderful spectator sport. Especially if you enjoy watching two supremely fit athletes, patiently waging battles of attrition from the baseline, grunting, sprinting and sliding through clouds of brick dust, waiting for the precise moment to go in for the kill. In this regard, few players put on a better show than Rafa Nadal.

On the ATP tour, clay-court tournaments are first staged in February and March, during the South American summer, currently in Brazil, Argentina and Chile. Then the focus switches to Europe, when hotel washing machines in some of the continent's finest cities whirr into overdrive as they attempt to rinse the red brick dust from players' kit. There are currently events in Marbella, Cagliari, Monte Carlo, Barcelona, Belgrade (twice), Munich, Estoril, Madrid, Rome, Geneva, Lyon, Parma and Paris – the latter for Roland Garros, the clay-court Grand Slam event. (There are also tournaments in the Moroccan city of Marrakech and the Texan city of Houston, plus five European tournaments after Roland Garros, in Hamburg, Bastad, Umag, Gstaad and Kitzbuhel.)

LEFT: The Monte-Carlo Country Club, where Rafa has triumphed a record 11 times.

The hosting clubs and cities wax and wane according to the fortunes and nationalities of the world's top players, which explains why in 2021 there were two tournaments in Belgrade (the Serbia Open and the Belgrade Open), cashing in on the fame of Serbia's most famous son, Novak Djokovic. However, there are four clay-court tournaments that shine brightest and reddest of all, and these are the ones that all players want to excel in.

First is the Monte-Carlo Masters, in Monaco (well, technically just across the border in the French town of Roquebrune-Cap-Martin) in April, generally considered the season opener, even though there are minor tournaments the week before. With its steep, hillside location, and stunning views onto the glistening Mediterranean, the Monte-Carlo Country Club provides a beautiful backdrop to

some often beautiful tennis. Should you ever tire of watching the players, you can always switch your attention to the opulent locals swanning around the club in their designer clothing, yachts sometimes moored in the harbour. Monaco has been described as the land of "the haves and have-yachts" and Rafa has won the title there 11 times, more than any other player.

Next are the Madrid Open and the Rome Masters, played out in their country's capital cities in May. The former is staged at La Caja Magica (The Magic Box), in a linear park called Manzanares Park, in the San Fermin quarter. Rafa has triumphed here five times, again more than any other player.

The Rome Masters takes place at perhaps the most distinctive venue on the whole continent – Foro Italico, with its classic Italian fascist architecture from the Mussolini period. Featuring amphitheatre seating and imposing classical statues, it harks back to ancient Rome, imbuing matches with a truly gladiatorial spirit. Rafa has won here a record-breaking 10 times, yet again more than any other player in history.

But, in reality, Monte Carlo, Madrid and Rome are just dress rehearsals for the main act when, at the end of May, the world's top players all head for Paris to contest the clay season finale, Roland Garros (otherwise known as the French Open). For sheer scale and spectacle, France's Grand Slam is unmissable. Following recent renovations, the Stade Roland Garros, on the western edge of the French capital in the 16th arrondissement, is a 12.5-hectare complex, featuring three stadium courts – Court Philippe Chatrier (15,000 capacity), Court Suzanne Lenglen (10,000 capacity) and Court Simonne Mathieu (5,000 capacity) – and a further 15 exterior courts.

Named after a famous aviator from the First World War, whose friend built the original stadium, Roland Garros has seen substantial modernisation over the last few years. The latest addition, due for completion in time for the 2024 Olympic tennis tournament, is a retractable roof over Court Suzanne Lenglen.

The courts at Roland Garros are constructed with engineering prowess to rival that of a major road builder. Deep layers of gravel, clinker and crushed white limestone stretch far underground, all topped with a couple of millimetres of brick dust, giving the courts their distinctive ochre hue.

"Of all the playing surfaces offered in this sport, clay is both the most physically demanding and the most technically subtle," states the official Roland Garros website. "It's a combination that, without doubt, explains why Roland Garros was – until the arrival of the king of clay, Rafa Nadal – the toughest tournament for any player to dominate long-term."

And Rafa's domination really has been long-term. He has hoisted the men's singles trophy here, the Coupe des Mousquetaires (The Musketeers' Cup), above his shoulders a record 13 times, first in 2005 and most recently in 2020. No one is even close to emulating this record. It's highly unlikely anyone ever will. In fact, the nearest is Frenchman Max Decugis, with eight titles, but he was competing prior to the First World War when the event was known as the French Championships, and only members of French tennis clubs were allowed to compete. Other than Decugis, the next greatest champion is Sweden's Bjorn Borg, with six singles titles in the 1970s and early 1980s.

Julien Pichené and Christophe Thoreau are authors of an encyclopedia on Roland Garros entitled *Dicoculture Illustré de Roland Garros*. Here's what they say about Rafa's dominance there: "Indeed, this tremendous hard-worker, both a perfectionist and an insatiable player, appears to be the total, all-round champion. Amalgamated within him, you'll find all the most remarkable qualities of former Roland Garros winners: the consistency of Bjorn Borg, the scientific game of Ivan Lendl, the patience of Mats Wilander, the left arm of Guillermo Vilas, the bounding topspin of Sergi Bruguera, and the power of Jim Courier. What's more, he seems to have a Thomas Muster in each of his legs."

Despite the hyperbole, it's a compliment that isn't overstated. Simply look at Rafa's Roland Garros match record. He has contested a total of 108 matches, losing only three of them. It's a truly extraordinary achievement.

The French Open may not be the most famous of tennis's four Grand Slams – that honour certainly goes to Wimbledon. Nor is it the most exciting – for sheer adrenalin, the loud and rowdy US Open in New York City wins hands down. But Roland Garros possesses a certain style and panache that the other three don't have. This is Paris, after all.

When the world's greatest descend on the French capital, there's always a distinct sense of Gallic flair in the springtime air. The global pandemic inevitably dampened the party somewhat, but in normal years this stadium complex is the city of Paris encapsulated inside a single tennis club. Inside the vast rectangular Stade Roland Garros, tree-shaded promenades stretch out in a network across the complex, linking up the various courts and ornamental gardens. This being France, the food on offer is far better than at the other Grand Slams, as is the wine, obviously. And the spectators tend to be dressed more elegantly.

On the clay, though, when the matches commence, all elegance is quickly abandoned. Of all the surfaces, clay court tennis requires the most physicality.

What makes it so demanding is the length of the rallies. None of that short, sharp brutality you see on fast courts. On the red stuff it's quite normal to witness points lasting 15 shots – sometimes much longer – during which combatants must gradually and tactically jockey into a position from where they can execute a winner. "Playing on clay is like playing chess," was another of José Higueras's verdicts. "You have more time to be creative and more choices to make on what shots to hit."

Ground into a fine powder, the top layer of red clay courts gives the ball extra grip when it lands, holding on to it longer than a grass or hard court would, and slowing it down slightly. Because clay is softer than hard courts, more of the ball's energy is absorbed by the court. According to one survey, tennis balls retain just 59 per cent of their speed after bouncing on clay, compared to 60 per cent on acrylic hard courts and 70 per cent on grass. If there's moisture on the clay – often the case in Europe's more northern cities – this will slow the balls even more. The extra grip also means balls struck with heavy topspin have more kick after the bounce, often jumping up above an opponent's head. Rafa is particularly effective in this regard on his groundstrokes.

BELOW: Rafa takes on Roger Federer on Roland Garros's Court Philippe Chatrier in 2019.

> **He hits the heaviest shot in tennis. The ball jumps at a tough angle. His forehand is just ridiculous.**

Andy Murray

Clay-court specialists adopt techniques and tactics specific to clay. A major consideration is the ball trajectory. To make use of the extra spin that clay imparts on the ball, players hit heavy topspin shots. Slice shots are effective, too, especially on the backhand, keeping the ball really low to the ground, thereby preventing opponents from attacking with their return shot.

Footwork on clay is almost an art form, a ballet even. Many Mediterranean and South American players spend years perfecting the way they slide across the court. Essentially there are two types of slide. The first is before players hit their shot, where they run towards the ball, slide, balance and then strike the ball. The second is after players hit their shot, where the ball is coming so fast that they're forced to strike it on the run, then slide afterwards in order to skid, change directions, and get back into the recovery position quickly.

Tactical movement behind the baseline is vital. On hard and grass courts players can often stay close to the baseline during rallies, if they wish to. On clay, the extra kick on the groundstrokes forces them to run forwards to strike balls on the half-volley, or backwards to compensate for the really high-bouncing balls.

Dropshots are far more common in clay-court tennis than on other surfaces. It's not necessarily because the bounce is

LEFT: Rafa has perfected the art of sliding on clay.

NADAL'S WIN/LOSS RECORDS ON CLAY

Rafa Nadal's win/loss ratio in Grand Slam finals on all surfaces is 72.4%, having won 21 and lost 8. This is his record in the top clay tournaments:

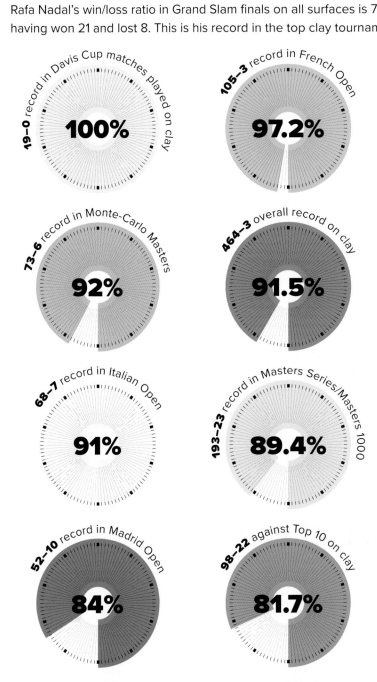

19–0 record in Davis Cup matches played on clay — **100%**

105–3 record in French Open — **97.2%**

73–6 record in Monte-Carlo Masters — **92%**

464–3 overall record on clay — **91.5%**

68–7 record in Italian Open — **91%**

193–23 record in Masters Series/Masters 1000 — **89.4%**

52–10 record in Madrid Open — **84%**

98–22 against Top 10 on clay — **81.7%**

HEAD TO HEAD ON CLAY

Rafa Nadal's win record on clay against players who have beaten him at least once.

Wins and losses

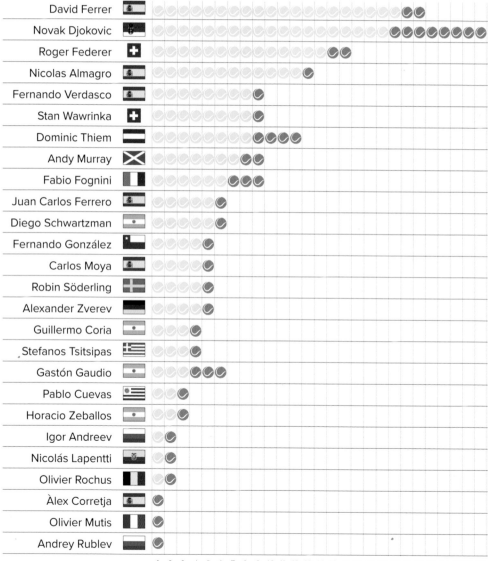

lower. It's more the fact that, with opponents often camped out deep behind their baselines, they naturally have further to run to the net in order to reach a dropshot.

And what about physical fitness? Clay-court matches usually last far longer than grass- or hard-court matches, sometimes beyond three hours. The toll on the legs can be brutal, as evidenced by the number of players who suffer cramps on this surface.

The equipment of a clay-court specialist differs slightly. Most important is the racket stringing. Some professional players use rougher strings on clay that grip the ball longer and allow them to give it more topspin. Or they opt for stronger, thicker-gauged strings that let them impart more spin and power, without sending the ball long. Some even drop their string tension ever so slightly in order to get more power for those big topspin shots.

Hitting extra spin moves the strings much more within the stringbed, with particles of brick dust lodging between strings and causing abrasion. This inevitably leads to more string breakages. At professional level it's quite normal to see a player break half a dozen or more strings during a single match.

ABOVE LEFT AND RIGHT: Specialist clay-court shoes offer grip on the surface but are designed not to clog up with clay.

OVERLEAF: In action at the 2019 French Open.

On clay players also wear specific shoes, normally with a herringbone pattern on the sole. This gives enough grip, allows for sliding, and crucially doesn't clog up too much with clay. But there's always a bit of extra clay that sticks around, so that it's normal for players to knock the soles of their shoes with their rackets to dislodge any remnants inside the grips.

And don't expect players to leave the court post-match without a bit of the red stuff on their clothing. Take a tumble and they may well end up covered in it.

Dirty clothes; dirty shoes; long, tough rallies; tired, cramped legs. Yes, clay is the surface players most suffer on. And those, like Rafa, who can endure the greatest amount of suffering end up being the most successful of all. As Rafa once explained: "I learned during my career to enjoy suffering."

THE MATCH

MONTE-CARLO MASTERS

April 17th, 2005
Monte-Carlo Country Club, Roquebrune-Cap-Martin, France
Final: Rafa Nadal vs. Guillermo Coria
Rafa Nadal beat Guillermo Coria 6–3, 6–1, 0–6, 7–5

// Rafael represents a new generation, a new wave." Wise words from the tournament director at the Monte-Carlo Masters in 2005 when he discovered the 18-year-old Mallorcan had reached the final at the Monte-Carlo Country Club.

Rafa's route to that final had impressed everyone. For the first four rounds, against Gael Monfils, Xavier Malisse, Olivier Rochus and Gaston Gaudio, he managed to avoid dropping a single set. Against Gaudio, the world number six and reigning French Open champion, in the quarter-finals, he was in demolishing form, winning 6-3, 6-0. What damage could he wreak in the final against Guillermo Coria?

This accomplished Argentinean, whose nickname was El Mago, or The Magician, had reached the final of the French Open the previous year, and had been as high as world number three. But ever since his ban in 2001 for testing positive for nandrolone (an infraction he blamed on a contaminated vitamin supplement), the clay-courter had been prone to nervousness at key moments in matches.

Rafa rampaged through the first two sets, increasingly turning up the pressure. As *The Guardian* newspaper's correspondent Stephen Bierley wrote: "Once at an opponent's throat, Nadal is a fearsome sight. His game is far from complete, but he has immense speed and a ferocious forehand, together with a lack of inhibition."

Nadal quickly had the first two sets done and dusted, 6–3, 6–1. But then, inexplicably, his concentration dropped and the momentum of the match swung the other way. In just half an hour he had lost the third set to love.

Coria must have thought he was in with a chance to turn the match around. Rafa proved he was made of sterner stuff, though. Quickly regrouping, he took control of the fourth set. Dressed in his three-quarter-length Capri trousers, white headband, and an orange sleeveless top that often camouflaged him against the

background of the court, he quickly found himself 1–0 up with a break point against Coria's serve. Nowadays we all know that, in situations like this, Rafa would close in for the kill with merciless ease. But back then tennis fans – and Coria it seemed – still didn't realise what this young man was capable of. A ten-shot rally ensued, with Rafa increasing the power of his groundstrokes and the volume of his grunting all the way through it. On shot six, he pushed Coria back with a deep cross-court backhand, followed by a blistering forehand down the

line, until finally he closed out the point with the most delicate of dropshots.

At two games to love and 40–30 up there came one of the most exhilarating points of the match. For 15 shots the two players traded textbook baseline groundstrokes, each waiting for the other to make an error. Then, on the 16th, Coria decided to throw in a surprising dropshot – and an effective one that would have flummoxed most players. But Rafa had anticipated it, and he sprinted forwards, popping the forehand down the line. Coria intercepted easily, returning the ball deep into the far corner, as far away from Nadal as he possibly could. Demonstrating his supreme fitness, Rafa then sprinted back, barely catching the ball to send it back down the line to Coria who, by this stage, was so worn down that he fluffed his final shot into the net.

Eventually Rafa had his match-point opportunity. But it required another lengthy rally – this time 16 shots – for him to secure victory in his first ever Masters Series tournament. Delighted, he fell back onto the court in celebration.

"Now is unbelievable. Today I am very, very concentrate. I am very concentrate all the time," he said after the match in his charmingly faltering English. "Yeah, yeah, my first very important tournament, no? All [will] remember this title, everything. But my objective is [to] improve my tennis. I need [to] improve my serve, my volley, my slice. And if I do, if I improve these shots, I think I can win a lot of matches, no?"

It was quite the understatement. That year, Rafa added three more Masters Series trophies to his cabinet, as well as his first Grand Slam title at Roland Garros. By the end of the season he had a total of 12 ATP tournament wins to his name.

LEFT: Rafa's 2005 campaign at the Monte-Carlo Masters included this semi-final victory over local hero Richard Gasquet.

RITUALS AND FEARS

_II_ I'm not superstitious, otherwise I would change the rituals with each defeat. I'm not even a slave to routine. What people call tics or rituals are how I put my head in order, because my head is normally very messy. It's a way to concentrate and silence the voices within. So I don't have to listen to the voice that tells me I'm going to lose; nor to the voice that, even more dangerously, tells me I'm going to win."

This was Rafa in a recent interview with Italian newspaper _Corriere dello Sport_, explaining for perhaps the thousandth time why he observes so many strictly defined rituals before and during his matches. An intriguing part of his character, these rituals are myriad in number and, from the outside at least, serve little obvious purpose.

Over the years, they have varied, depending on Rafa's state of mind, but they follow a general pattern.

It all starts in the locker room. He admits that, 45 minutes before matches start, he has to take a freezing-cold shower, in order to activate his concentration and ready his body for the battle ahead. Then he insists on applying the grips to all six rackets he normally takes on court. It has been reported that he refuses to wear socks higher than 15cm above his shoes; and that he pulls his bandana out of his kitbag an hour before play, but won't wrap it about his head until minutes before he walks on court, always tying it slowly, tightly, precisely. Often, he will refresh the bandana on court, tying it in the same concentrated, methodical way. He'll do aggressive jumps and sprints on the spot, listening to music. Then he takes a toilet break. He has admitted he often takes five or six "nervous pees" in the final hour before the match starts.

LEFT: Rafa finds comfort in lining up his water bottles with pinpoint precision.

Then follow a plethora of pre-match rituals. In the major tournaments, where ball boys and girls carry players' kitbags onto court as a courtesy, Rafa insists on keeping hold of one racket himself. Once arrived at his courtside chair, he normally requires his bag to be placed neatly next to his chair. (At one point it had to have a towel positioned beneath it.) Now for the water bottles: always two, one filled with cold water, the other at room temperature, lined up meticulously on the floor, in front of his chair, to the left, with the labels facing diagonally towards the court. At changes of end, you'll notice he always sips from each bottle.

With the warm-up complete, Rafa prefers to remain seated in his chair longer than his opponent – always the last man sitting. But then there's a sudden burst of action as he makes his exaggerated sprint to the baseline before the commencement of hostilities. In between points he adjusts his gait in order not to step on the lines of the court. When a game ends, he always allows his opponent to walk past the netpost to his chair before he passes it himself.

There are some further things to be done before the serve: adjust sweatbands, adjust headband, adjust shirt, tuck hair behind ears, bounce ball a precise number of times. A familiar sequence after he reaches the baseline and receives tennis balls would be: a quick tug at the underpants through his shorts with his right hand, pull the left shoulder of his shirt up, the right shoulder of his shirt up, touch his nose, tuck hair behind each ear then start bouncing the ball. The shorts and shirt tugs have nothing to do with inferior clothing – after all, his sponsors have spent millions developing some of the world's best tennis kit. It's just another one of his calming, centring routines. He has said he's not even aware that, live in front of thousands of spectators, and millions more worldwide on TV, he attempts to pull his underpants up through his shorts before every service; often a second time between first serve and second serve. "I've been doing that since I was a kid, so that's something that I cannot change," he told GQ magazine. "It's just something that's impossible for me to change. I can change many things, but this thing, no."

Even his poor mother Ana Maria has been drawn into the great debate. "You don't know how many pairs of underwear people have given him believing that the ones he has do not fit well," she once revealed in a Spanish magazine. "One person sent me a letter saying we should shop for larger sizes and enclosed four pairs. It's a nervous tic and the more nervous he is ... He has had it all his life. I think that he has a bottom a bit bigger than he should have."

Not that Rafa is the only tennis player to display a sequenced ritual before

serving. Alexander Zverev pulls his T-shirt up to scratch an imaginary itch before serving, while Denis Shapovalov bounces the ball twice between his legs. Novak Djokovic's ball bouncing, both with his racket and hand, can be interminable. He once admitted his record was 38 times, during a Davis Cup match.

It's true to say that irrational or superstitious routines and rituals can play a big part in sports psychology, where success comes from belief. During his 2001 Wimbledon campaign, Croatian player Goran Ivanisevic, another left-hander, convinced himself that watching the children's TV programme *Teletubbies* every day would help him win. (And he did.) And in 2008, when favourite Serena Williams was defeated in the third round of the French Open, she blamed her shock exit on a failure to stick to familiar routines. "I didn't tie my laces right and I didn't bounce the ball five times and I didn't bring my shower sandals to the court with me," she said. "I didn't have my extra dress. I just knew it was fate. It wasn't going to happen."

Athletes in other sports can be even more bafflingly superstitious. Take English cricketer Mark Ramprakash, for example. In 2011 he attributed his run of good batting to chewing the same piece of chewing gum. If the day's play had ended and he was still not out, he would stick the gum to the end of his bat handle, "for when I resume my innings the next morning", he said.

Australian football goalkeeper Mark Schwarzer wore the same pair of shinpads for his entire professional career. First, in 1990, at the age of 19, and then for every match until he retired in 2016. "I had to tell the kit man at various clubs: 'If you lose those I'll kill you'," he once explained.

Tiger Woods famously wears a red shirt on the final round of his golfing competitions, something he's done ever since he was a junior. "I just stuck with it out of superstition, and it worked. It's not going to change."

But is there a method to all this superstitious madness? One American psychologist back in the 1940s suggested that, in order to understand human superstition, we needed to take a lesson from our feathered friends. In 1947 Burrhus Frederic Skinner, a behavioural psychologist from Indiana University (and later professor of psychology at Harvard University), carried out an experiment with pigeons. He placed hungry birds inside a cage attached to a device that automatically delivered food. Bizarrely, the pigeons quickly started associating food with whatever random actions they had been performing when it was delivered to them, and subsequently believed that repeating these random actions would result in more food.

"One bird was conditioned to turn counter-clockwise about the cage, making two or three turns between reinforcements," Skinner wrote in the *Journal of Experimental Psychology*, under the title "Superstition in the Pigeon". "Another repeatedly thrust its head into one of the upper corners of the cage. A third developed a 'tossing' response, as if placing its head beneath an invisible bar and lifting it repeatedly. Two birds developed a pendulum motion of the head and body, in which the head was extended forward and swung from right to left with a sharp movement followed by a somewhat slower return."

All of which makes Rafa's water bottle placement, cold showers and underpant-pulling suddenly seem less comedic.

Skinner compared pigeon superstitions with human superstitions in the following way: "The experiment might be said to demonstrate a sort of superstition. The bird behaves as if there were a causal relation between its behaviour and the presentation of food, although such a relation is lacking. There are many analogies in human behaviour. Rituals for changing one's luck at cards are good examples. A few accidental connections between a ritual and favourable consequences suffice to set up and maintain the behaviour in spite of many unreinforced instances. The bowler who has released a ball down the alley but continues to behave as if he were controlling it by twisting and turning his arm and shoulder is another case in point. These behaviours have, of course, no real effect

LEFT: Tucking back stray hairs before serving is another key ritual.

upon one's luck or upon a ball halfway down an alley, just as in the present case the food would appear as often if the pigeon did nothing – or, more strictly speaking, did something else."

So while Rafa's rituals and routines have no real effect on the outcome of a match, they do serve to calm his mind. Subconsciously he believes they have an effect. The control he exerts over these rituals helps him counter the lack of control he has over other elements of the match. "When I do these things it means I am focused, I am competing," he once explained. "It's something I don't need to do but when I do it, it means I'm focused."

Rafa has talked about his need to become a "tennis machine" during matches, by bottling up his feelings, fighting back against his vulnerabilities and thereby increasing his chances of winning. This, he says, is his version of a medieval knight going into battle in a suit of armour. "It's a kind of self-hypnosis, a game you play, with deadly seriousness, to disguise your own weaknesses from yourself, as well as from your rival," he explains in his autobiography *Rafa: My Story*.

Then there's the thorny question of his phobias. Over the years he has admitted to more than a few irrational fears. His mother has described how he is scared of the dark and prefers to sleep with the lights on. She once revealed how her son called her up in the middle of the night in a panic. "He called me and said, 'Mum, we have a problem'," she remembers. "'There's a power failure and I'm scared to death.' I had to tell him which drawer the batteries for the torches were in."

In an interview with *Vogue* magazine, Rafa explained his fear of the dark. "Being home alone at night makes me a bit nervous. If I'm at home I have to sleep on the sofa. I can't face going to bed. I'm there with the TV on and all the lights on. I'm not very brave about anything in life. In tennis, yes. In everything else, not very."

As a youngster, during thunderstorms, Rafa would cower beneath cushions. Even as an adult, his mother says, he tries to stop his family from heading outside when there's thunder and lightning forecast. When he was very small, this fear of storms was a trait Uncle Toni used to turn to his advantage in order to persuade his nephew to concentrate on the court. He told Rafa that if he didn't focus 100 per cent on his game, the thunder gods would get irate. The ploy worked every time.

But fear of thunderstorms is just the tip of the iceberg. Fast cars, motorcycles, helicopters, bicycles, deep water, house fires, dogs, spiders, in fact most animals... a whole litany of everyday things and occurrences fill him with dread.

The fact he is "terrified" by helicopters is perhaps understandable. However, if there is a professional need to travel in a helicopter, he will. He tries to avoid

ABOVE AND OVERLEAF: While Rafa's rituals have no effect on the outcome of the match, they do serve to calm his mind.

motorcycles, too. "I have a motorbike, but it was a present and I do not use it," he once said. "I don't ride it. I am scared about motorcycles. That's very dangerous. We only have one life."

Less understandable, though, is his fear of driving, especially when you consider he has owned several very powerful sports cars. His mother points out how cautious her son is behind the wheel, constantly braking and accelerating, and always nervous about overtaking.

For an island boy, the fear of deep water seems illogical, too. Yet Rafa's sister once revealed how her brother wouldn't jet-ski or swim in the ocean unless he could see the sea floor (something that he must have come to terms with, given the paparazzi photos of him jet-skiing with his wife and friends); and diving off high rocks, a stunt favoured by many kids across Mallorca, is completely off limits. What about bikes? He says he was never comfortable riding a bicycle, always worried he would fall off.

SINGLES SERVICE AND RETURN RECORD

	2005	2008	2013
Singles Service Record			
Aces	219	283	221
Double Faults	131	117	120
1st Serve	69%	69%	69%
1st Serve Points Won	71%	72%	73%
2nd Serve Points Won	57%	60%	57%
Break Points Faced	449	395	356
Break Points Saved	64%	67%	69%
Service Games Played	1,038	1,054	913
Service Games Won	84%	88%	88%
Total Service Points Won	66%	68%	68%
Singles Return Record			
1st Serve Return Points Won	37%	34%	35%
2nd Serve Return Points Won	57%	55%	54%
Break Points Opportunities	845	786	662
Break Points Converted	46%	45%	47%
Return Games Played	1,031	1,045	916
Return Games Won	38%	33%	34%
Return Points Won	45%	43%	42%
Total Points Won	55%	55%	55%

2017	2020	2005 – 2020 Comparison	Career All Surfaces	Career Clay
286	157		3,782	957
123	66		2,002	652
68%	64%		68%	70%
74%	75%		72%	70%
61%	58%		57%	57%
340	160		6,168	2,456
70%	68%		67%	67%
939	414		14,491	5,334
89%	87%		86%	85%
70%	69%		67%	66%
35%	35%		34%	40%
56%	57%		55%	58%
718	278		10,713	4,656
41%	49%		45%	49%
908	398		14,352	5,272
33%	34%		34%	43%
43%	43%		42%	47%
56%	56%		55%	56%

Rafa's greatest fear of all, it seems, is that some terrible fate might befall his family. The remote possibility of illness or accident puts him in a tailspin. His mother remembers how, during the colder months, Rafa would constantly remind his mother to check the fire in the fireplace was fully extinguished before going to bed. If he headed out for the evening with his friends, he would sometimes phone her three times to remind her. There's no overstating the closeness of the bonds with his family. Perhaps this explains why he has never moved away from his island home. Many of his tennis-playing peers have relocated to various tax havens around the world, while Rafa would rather stay close to his family, despite a top rate of personal income tax in Spain of 47 per cent.

The global Covid pandemic added to Rafa's fears, just as it did to almost everyone else's. Aged 33 when it first struck, he says he wasn't fearful for his own health. "However, if I get infected, I can infect people at risk," he explained in a recent interview. "I am worried for my parents, for my family, for my community. It is the hardest time in our life. This is why it is time to fight for things that are much more important than a tennis match."

Watch Rafa on court, and all these rituals, routines and phobias make for a compelling spectacle. Seeing that combination of finely honed athlete and scared little boy is an intriguing view deep into the man's soul.

Rafa's coach Carlos Moya has compared his charge to the dual personality of Clark Kent and Superman – the mild-mannered, bespectacled, socially awkward nerd who, at the flick of a switch, metamorphoses into the fearless, athletic, triumphant superhero. Like Superman, Rafa always displays simultaneously aspects of both his mild-mannered homeboy and his superhero.

As he has himself explained: "On the tennis courts, maybe on the outside I look fearless, but on the inside, I'm scared. I think fear is a part of life."

SERVICE DIRECTION: RAFA NADAL'S SERVING PATTERNS

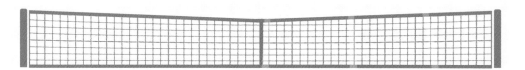

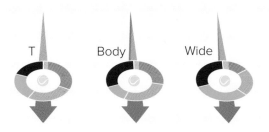

T   Body   Wide

Nadal First-
Serve Direction
Love-all
Wide = **25%**
Body = **13%**
T   = **62%**

Nadal First-
Serve Direction
15–15
Wide = **36%**
Body = **13%**
T   = **51%**

Nadal First-
Serve Direction
30–0
Wide = **52%**
Body = **6%**
T   = **42%**

Nadal First-
Serve Direction
0–30
Wide = **49%**
Body = **14%**
T   = **37%**

TOP LEFT: A nervous Rafa takes a rare helicopter ride in Perth, Australia, in 2020.

TOP RIGHT: Facing the media during the global pandemic.

OVERLEAF: Competing in Miami, Florida, in 2004.

"Somewhere there is a Planet Nadal where babies don't play with dolls but with rackets; where muscle grows before bone, where courage is learned before speech, and the heart beats faster. Rafa is an adolescent who has transformed himself into a superman."

El Pais newspaper

THE MATCH

FRENCH OPEN

June 5th 2005

Stade Roland Garros, Paris, France

Final: Rafa Nadal vs. Mariano Puerta

Rafa Nadal beat Mariano Puerta 6–7, 6–3, 6–1, 7–5

When Rafa won his maiden title at Roland Garros aged just 19, who might have dared suggest he would be champion on the Paris clay a further 12 times, more than any other player in history? With hindsight, we now accept this elite Spaniard as the unrivalled king of the red stuff, but back then, 13 French Open titles were unthinkable.

Throughout the late winter and spring of 2005, Rafa's level of play on clay courts had been rising exponentially. In February he'd won minor ATP tournaments in Brazil and Mexico. In early April, on hard courts, he reached the final of the Miami Masters, losing in a thrilling five-setter to Roger Federer. Later that month, back on clay, he won his first ATP Masters event at Monte Carlo, and then further titles in Barcelona and Rome.

By the time he reached the final at Roland Garros, having seen off Richard Gasquet, Sebastien Grosjean, David Ferrer and Roger Federer in earlier rounds, he looked unstoppable. Up against Argentina's Mariano Puerta, on Court Phillipe Chatrier, he was expected by the vast majority of fans to secure a Spanish victory. Among those fans was Juan Carlos I, the King of Spain. The fact that the monarch of Spain had travelled to Paris to watch the fresh prince of clay-court tennis was testament to just how highly this young Mallorcan was rated.

Sporting shoulder-length hair, his trademark pirate-style trousers, a white headband and a lime-green sleeveless top, Rafa embarked on his first Grand Slam final with more than a little brio, breaking serve on the very first game. Then, with Rafa 3–1 and 40–15 up, Puerta called a halt, walked slowly over to his chair and requested the trainer strap up his right thigh. If Rafa might have suspected his first slam final was going to be all over within a quick half-hour, he was quickly disabused of such thoughts as Puerta saved two game points and broke back to level the game at 3–3. Despite the strapping, there was no sign of any weakness from the Argentinean. The two players continued to trade pugnacious groundstrokes, Puerta regularly battering his rival with venomous shots that should have had him flailing. Rafa's defensive play was sensational, though, as was his ability to switch instantly into counter-attack mode. And to the delight of the crowd, virtually all of his winning points were punctuated with a fist pump and a loud cry of "Vamos!" It's a celebration we are now all accustomed to but, back then, in the early days of his career, this supreme confidence still jarred. Puerta seemed to react to it with a combination of disgruntlement and bemusement. But then again, he had called a time-out.

BELOW: Puerta and Rafa embark on the 2005 French Open final.

This first-set battle soon advanced to a tiebreak, perhaps the most crucial point of which came at 2–2 when an intense 14-shot rally ended with Rafa chasing down a dropshot and Puerta defending the net. Rafa then duly slammed his return straight at his opponent's head, before celebrating with yet another fist pump. To be fair, he did apologise briefly afterwards but you could tell the tension between the two players was now hotter than ever.

Fired up, Rafa then hit two astounding winners, a looping forehand into the corner and a backhand down the line that astounded everyone, not least Rafa himself who dropped his racket in astonishment. Teasing the Spaniard with dropshots, Puerta reacted and managed to jockey himself into set-point position at 6–5. And then again at 7–6, before winning the tiebreak to take the first set.

Rafa's response was swift and devastating. For the first time in this tournament, he found himself a set down. Sinking into despondency had never been his style, however, and he dialled up the pressure, chasing down balls that lesser players would have given up on. It all made for some thrilling exchanges, and a match that many still consider a clay-court classic.

In the fourth game of that second set, Rafa broke Puerta's serve again. After that, the Argentinean, who had survived five-set matches in the quarter-finals and semi-finals, found his resolve slipping. Rafa then dominated much of the third set, too, winning it thanks to a double fault from his opponent.

From somewhere, however, Puerta discovered a reserve of energy. At 5–4 and 40–15 up in the fourth set, he found himself with two set points, both of which were frustrated by athletic responses from the Spaniard. A third set point was repelled, too, so that suddenly, instead of stretching out the match to a fifth set, Puerta was now facing break point himself. Rafa pulled back to 5–5.

Puerta had missed his chance – 5–6 and 30–40 down, serving to stay in the match, he eventually folded, sending a forehand wide. Rafa instantly dropped down, flat on his back, exhausted yet elated. The king of clay's reign had begun.

But in the meantime there was the King of Spain to attend to. Rafa, his hair, shirt and shorts streaked with brick dust, climbed into the stands to embrace his parents, sister, uncles, aunts, support team and close friends. Juan Carlos then leant down from the president's box to congratulate his loyal subject, grasping him by his sweaty biceps – the very muscle that had inflicted so much damage on Puerta. Emotional and tearful, Rafa waited patiently in his chair, courtside, while the trophy ceremony was prepared. Finally, accompanied by one of the ball girls, he made the long walk to the podium.

OPPOSITE TOP:
Rafa's exuberant celebrations are now second nature, but at the 2005 French Open opponents found them jarring.

OPPOSITE BOTTOM:
Uncle Toni and Juan Carlos I, King of Spain, congratulate a new national hero.

It was the legendary French footballer Zinedine Zidane who handed him the Coupe des Mousquetaires trophy.

That night, Rafa and his team celebrated the victory in a nightclub on the Champs Elysées. Meanwhile congratulations were arriving from all quarters. Spanish politicians were quick to jump on the patriotic bandwagon. His official website was bombarded with messages, including several offers of marriage.

Years later, Rafa looked back on his maiden Grand Slam triumph with extreme fondness. "I was very young. I had tremendous energy, the impulse of youth," he reminisced. "I was capable of returning tough shots, of winning important points, and of returning these shots with strength and power. I played with true passion. I played a good match during the semi-final, and the final wasn't an easy match. But physically I felt great. I was confident with my game because I had won all the previous tournaments [that spring] but I was well aware that anything could happen.

"It all happened so quickly. I went from being number 50 in the world to competing in the final of Roland Garros in two months. I handled it well, with serenity. I had the right upbringing. I had been prepared to handle such an event. After that victory I came back to the hotel and I said: 'Okay, I won the most important thing that I can win in tennis. So then I'm going to play with less pressure, more calm the rest of my career.' The real thing is completely the opposite: every year you play with more and more pressure."

RIGHT: French football legend Zinedine Zidane presents Rafa with his first Roland Garros trophy.

> The truth is that it [biting trophies] all started as a joke. But from then on there were always photographers who were asking me to do it. I kept doing it and now I have no option but to go on doing so because I can assure you that they don't taste good.

Rafa Nadal

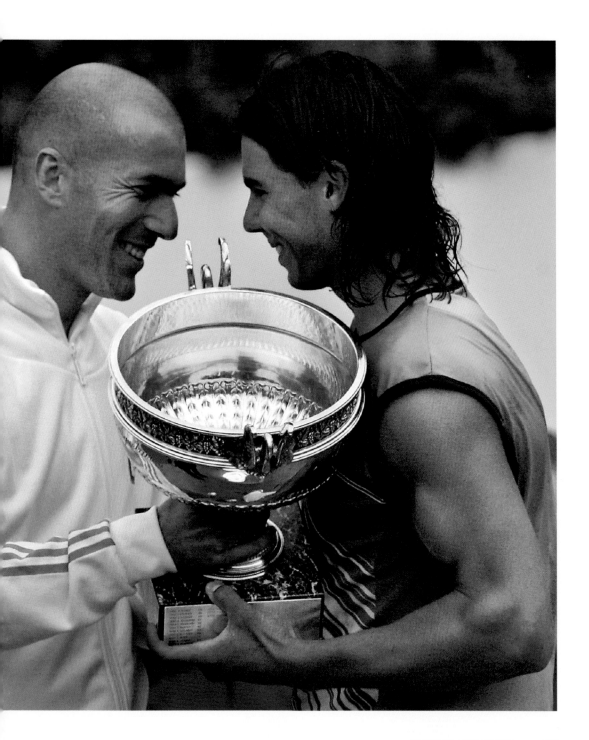

6

MAKING MONEY

LEFT: Wearing Nike in Cincinnati – Shorts, tick; Wristbands, tick; T-shirt, tick; Headband, tick.

As he approaches the latter stages of his career, Rafa's earnings from prize money and sponsorship are diminishing. Back in 2014, the year he won his ninth French Open at Roland Garros, he earned a staggering US$44.5million, including $30million from sponsors and $14.5million from tournament winnings. By 2016 this had dropped slightly to a total of $37.5million. In 2018 it was back up to $41.4million.

Precisely how much sportsmen and women earn is an inexact science. Accountants are hardly likely to publish their clients' tax returns for all to see. However, every year, American business magazine *Forbes* publishes its list of the world's 50 highest-paid athletes, using research from industry insiders on prize money, salaries, bonuses, sponsorship deals, appearance fees, licensing income and business ventures. The list covering the period of May 2020 to May 2021, places Irish mixed martial arts fighter Conor McGregor at the very top, with total earnings of $180million. Soccer legends Lionel Messi and Cristiano Ronaldo are ranked second and third with $130million and $120million respectively. The highest-paid tennis player is Roger Federer with $90million. Rafa, though, who spent much of 2020 and 2021 sidelined either through injury or the global pandemic, is nowhere to be seen.

Not that he'll be tightening his belt any time soon. During the course of his long career, he has so far amassed around $127 million in match prize money alone – the third-highest male player of all time, behind Djokovic ($153 million) and Federer ($131 million). This is dwarfed, however, by the gargantuan sponsorship payments he has received. Since he turned professional in 2001, many different brands have rushed to be associated with this player, increasingly keen with every new Grand Slam title he adds to his haul. His latest roster of sponsors includes his long-time clothing brand Nike, his racket brand Babolat, plus Spanish financial giant Santander Group, car manufacturer Kia, Spanish insurance company Mapfre, Heliocare skincare products, Spanish telecoms company Telefonica, Swiss watch manufacturer Richard Mille and Dutch beer Amstel (the non-alcoholic version, of course).

Rafa is by no means the richest player to wield a tennis racket. That honour goes to Roger Federer. In 2020, according to *Forbes* magazine, he earned $106.3 million – more than any other athlete on the planet. As stated, the Swiss national is top-ranked among tennis players on the latest rich list with $90m, but in the ATP-logged calendar year of 2021 he only earned $647,655 of that in prize money. Roger was followed on the *Forbes* list by Naomi Osaka, Serena Williams and Djokovic.

So what is it about tennis that guarantees such huge sponsorship income for the top pros? It's mainly thanks to television. At tennis tournaments, in between points, the TV cameras focus on the players' faces and upper bodies, guaranteeing that clothing logos are regularly in shot. Matches can last three hours or more – especially on Rafa's favoured surface, clay – which, by the end of a tournament, adds up to a huge amount of on-screen exposure. Tennis is globally popular (the men's ATP tour stages events in over 30 nations on six continents), especially with the wealthy middle classes, and enjoys TV coverage from January to November. Sponsors earn a healthy return on their investments.

But the likes of Rafa, Federer and Djokovic have an extra draw: charisma, looks and widespread media appeal. In Rafa's case, he has been winning Grand Slam titles since 2005, guaranteeing him global media coverage and consequently household-name status. While he doesn't command half a dozen languages like Federer does, he does speak Mallorqui, Spanish and English, the latter albeit with some charming quirks. Spanish and English ensure his interviews are picked up in multiple territories all over the planet. He is good-looking, too, in a wholesome sort of way, and quite the clothes horse both on and off the court. In the past he has modelled – often stripped down to his underpants – for Emporio Armani and Tommy Hilfiger.

The majority of the brands that associate with him – undies notwithstanding – are fairly corporate in nature. This explains why he is always so ultra-cautious not to say anything controversial in interviews or on social media. One slip of the tongue or the thumb and he could lose a highly lucrative contract overnight. It's fair to say that many of Rafa's press conferences amount to nothing but long-winded exercises in the fine art of saying very little at all.

OPPOSITE TOP:
Babolat has rewarded Rafa handsomely over the years for his endorsement.

OPPOSITE BOTTOM:
At a sponsor's photo shoot for Spanish insurance company Mapfre.

There have been plenty of smaller sponsors, too, but hardly what you'd call blue chip. Biscuits, video games, gym equipment, and he must have got a good deal for his Sunreef catamaran, as he happily poses on the back for some of the company's promotional photos.

While some of the larger brands require personal appearances, TV adverts, social media campaigns, shirt patches and corporate glad-handing as part of the contractual deal, many of the smaller ones are happy to have brush-by contact, satisfied with perhaps a short press conference, a couple of media appearances, and a brief mention on social media channels.

His social media profile grows with every passing year. When this book was being prepared, he had a staggering 15.6 million followers on Twitter, 14 million on Facebook and 12.2 million on Instagram, much of the content on these channels dedicated to promoting his sponsors.

Rafa has even dipped his toe into the world of pop music. In 2010 he starred alongside Colombian singer Shakira in the video for her song "Gypsy". There was an English-language version as well as a Spanish version, "Gitana". In Spain the single went platinum, helped in no small way by Rafa's smouldering appearance in the dry desert heat.

The video kicks off with the Colombian, nine years Rafa's senior, playing a country music-style intro on the harmonica, while walking towards camera in a skimpy black halter top and skirt. Rafa meanwhile, all sweaty and sultry, waits patiently, like a lovelorn teenager, in jeans and white T-shirt, clinging on to a chain-link fence.

Now the footage cuts to both Latin lovers lying on the ground, holding hands, cuddling, rubbing noses and whispering sweet nothings to each other. Suddenly Rafa has his shirt off and Shakira's straddling him, stroking his hair. Then there's a hint of flamenco dancing from the Colombian, more cuddling, and a private dance for Rafa. It all ends with a final kiss.

While the video no doubt boosted Rafa's image, especially across the Spanish-speaking world, it's by no means an indication of a future career in acting. Besides, the tennis player has plenty of business interests to occupy his time once he retires from professional tennis.

As a younger man, he claimed to have no interest at all in amassing money. In the 2008 book *Rafael Nadal: Master on Clay* by Jaume Pujol-Galceran and Manel Serras, he explained how he would leave all the financial decisions to his father. "I haven't a clue how much money I earn. That's not to say I joke about money, but I've never had to take care of it. I only know that, by playing well, I won't have any money problems."

The cheap mobile phone he owned at the time was proof, he said, of his indifference to wealth. "Of all the Spanish players, I've got the ugliest phone. People often joke about me on the tour because of this telephone. All I care about is that it works. I don't need an ultra-modern device with a load of functions that I'll never use. Some people are happy just drinking a Coca-Cola at the seaside. That's me. Others need to drive a Ferrari or buy a private jet. Each to his own." Needless to say, nowadays he carries a far more expensive phone. Although he

BELOW: Luckily for Shakira, Rafa was very experienced at lying down and rolling around on a hot clay surface.

RAFA'S SUCCESS TIMELINE

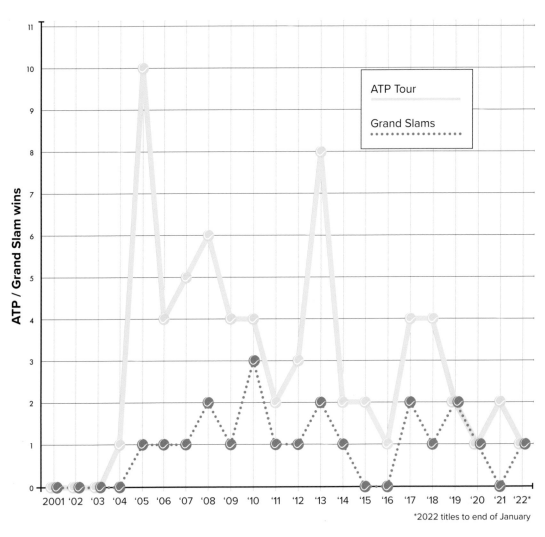

ATP / Grand Slam wins

ATP Tour

Grand Slams

2001 '02 '03 '04 '05 '06 '07 '08 '09 '10 '11 '12 '13 '14 '15 '16 '17 '18 '19 '20 '21 '22*

*2022 titles to end of January

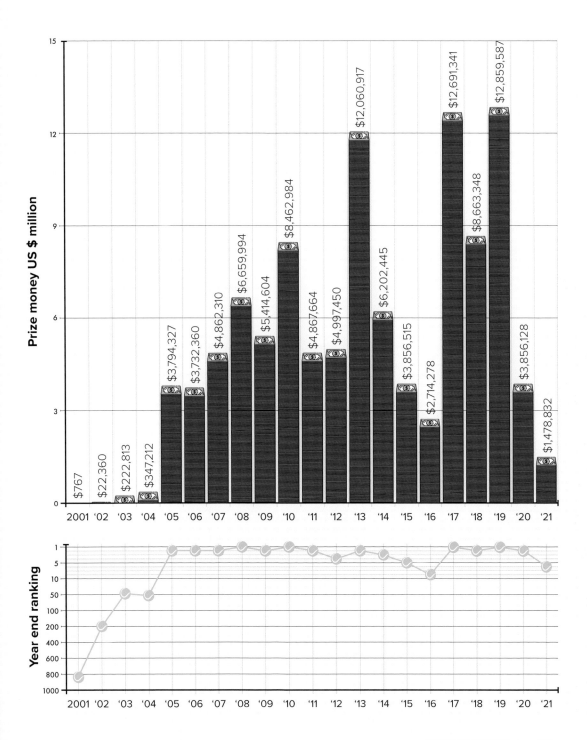

Prize money US $ million

$767
$22,360
$222,813
$347,212
$3,794,327
$3,732,360
$4,862,310
$6,659,994
$5,414,604
$8,462,984
$4,867,664
$4,997,450
$12,060,917
$6,202,445
$3,856,515
$2,714,278
$12,691,341
$8,663,348
$12,859,587
$3,856,128
$1,478,832

2001 '02 '03 '04 '05 '06 '07 '08 '09 '10 '11 '12 '13 '14 '15 '16 '17 '18 '19 '20 '21

Year end ranking

1
5
10
50
100
200
400
600
800
1000

2001 '02 '03 '04 '05 '06 '07 '08 '09 '10 '11 '12 '13 '14 '15 '16 '17 '18 '19 '20 '21

still often prefers to travel on normal aeroplanes (in business or first class) rather than private jets.

Over the years, Rafa and his family have built up an impressive business empire that now stretches all over Mallorca, Spain and even abroad. Even before he turned professional, his parents already operated several local businesses in Manacor and the surrounding area. His mother's family owned a furniture business in Manacor, a town where the furniture industry had been thriving for decades. It was thanks to Rafa's great-grandfather on his mother's side, who was a very skilled cabinetmaker, that the family business initially flourished. Rafa's grandfather once told him that in 1970, a total of 2,000 wooden beds were

BELOW: With DJ Krystal Roxx and TV presenter Laura Whitmore at a party sponsored by drinks brand Bacardi in 2013.

made across the Balearic Islands – half of them in his own workshops. That may be an exaggeration.

Later on, Rafa's mother, Ana María, owned and ran a perfume shop, which she gave up in order to focus on her role as mother and homemaker.

Rafa's father Sebastián is now one of the most successful and renowned businessmen on the entire island. According to his son, he is driven both by money and the thrill of the deal. He started working as a teenager, opening a bar at the beach resort in Porto Cristo. At 19 he sold used cars, before working in a bank for a short time. Then he moved into glass-making and glazing, just as Mallorca's tourism industry was really prospering in the early 1980s, accompanied by a construction boom that cried out for glass doors, windows and tables. After a couple of years, Sebastián and his brother Toni raised money to buy the glass-making company, now called Vidres Mallorca, outright. But it was Sebastián who operated it, leaving Toni time to coach his nephew.

From then on Sebastián and Toni's business empire flourished, initially expanding into property. For a long time, Toni took half the profits of the business, while doing virtually none of the work. The brothers were happy with the situation since Rafa's tennis coaching was progressing so impressively. At one point, Rafa, his father and his two uncles, Miguel Angel and Toni, established a company called Nadal Invest, focusing on property. All of Rafa's sponsorship deals were initially negotiated by his father, too.

Later, when Rafa started winning large amounts of prize money on the ATP tour, and even more from sponsorship and product endorsements, his father suggested the young player ought to pay Uncle Toni a salary for coaching services. It was an idea Toni immediately quashed, worried it would upset the equilibrium of their relationship. He was happy to receive money from his brother, but he certainly didn't want his nephew paying him since that would imply Rafa was his employer. Toni wanted to define his position as boss of their tennis relationship.

Rafa describes his father as a hard-working businessman who overcomes problems and gets the job done. There is some of that no-nonsense industry in Rafa's own attitude to tennis matches.

Nowadays, Sebastián sits atop a very successful business empire, with a portfolio of property, glass-making, insurance and restaurants. But investments stretch well beyond these fields, and well beyond Mallorca. He is one of the directors of Mabel Capital, a Madrid-based investment firm with over 300 employees that operates across Spain, Portugal, the UK and the United

States. Rafa himself reportedly owns a 33 per cent stake in the company, which includes operations in a vast array of fields including finance, property, hospitality, sport, media and music. There are residential and commercial property ventures in Madrid, Lisbon, the Costa del Sol, Philadelphia and Los Angeles. There's a food supplement brand called Earthbar. There are two chains of restaurants – one called Tatel, with premises in Madrid, Ibiza, Miami and Beverly Hills, which is co-owned by Portuguese footballer (and former Real Madrid player) Cristiano Ronaldo and Spanish singer Enrique Iglesias, and another called Zela.

In 2010 Rafa became a major shareholder in his beloved football club Real Madrid CF. His investment was seen as something of a lifeline for the La Liga club, which at the time, was drowning in debt. His second uncle Miguel Angel – no stranger to the turbulent world of professional football – was appointed as assistant coach for a while.

Another very important Nadal business venture is the Rafa Nadal Academy. (Or the Rafa Nadal Academy by Movistar, to use its full name.) Headed up by Uncle Toni, with fellow Spanish tennis players Carlos Moya and Carlos Costa acting as technical director and head of business respectively, this vast sports

franchise is headquartered in Manacor. There are swimming pools, at least 26 tennis courts, facilities for football and squash, an international school, a museum, a health clinic and a fitness centre. Sometimes Rafa can combine his business interests. When he took delivery of a brand new Kia EV6 electric car, the event took place at the Rafa Nadal Tennis Academy in Manacor. There are further tennis centres in the Mexican city of Cancun and the resort of Sani, in northern Greece. Courses are offered to both amateurs and budding professionals.

"For us, human training is equally as important as sports coaching and therefore our goal is for each player to be capable of putting values such as hard work, humility, tolerance, patience, respect, discipline and commitment into practice," Rafa says of his coaching philosophy.

The most recent facility to open under Rafa's brand is the Rafa Nadal Academy Kuwait. Housed at the Sheikh Jaber Al-Abdullah Al-Jaber Al-Sabah International Tennis Complex, this is the first facility of its kind in the Middle East, featuring 15 tennis courts, two squash courts, a swimming pool, a 1500-square-metre gym and a boxing ring. As well as a members' club, on offer there are tennis lessons, personal training, fitness classes, swimming classes and after-school programmes.

Courtesy of the Nadals, there is considerable philanthropic work, too, through the Fundación Rafa Nadal (Rafa Nadal Foundation). Rafa and his mother established the charity in 2008, focusing on helping underprivileged kids through sport and education, with various projects now operating in Spain, India and the United States. Their aim, they state, is to help children "reach the maximum of their possibilities, empowering them and fostering values such as self-improvement, respect and effort." Rafa's mother is president, his father vice-president, and his wife director. He is also alert to hardships on his own doorstep in Mallorca.

After torrential rain and flash flooding devastated the town of Llorenc des Cardassar in October 2018, with the death of 13 people and hundreds of homes and businesses swamped with dirty water, Rafa spent hours helping volunteers to clean up the area. He opened up rooms at the Rafa Nadal Academy for those who needed refuge and provided a donation of one million euros through his foundation.

OPPOSITE: At the opening of his Mexican tennis centre in Cancun in 2019.

ABOVE: Rafa's latest academy is in in Kuwait.

RIGHT: With Roger Federer at the opening of his academy in 2016.

Much of Rafa's business is instantly recognisable thanks to the personal logo he uses to market it – two symmetrical bull horns and thunderbolts, a reference to his raging bull playing style.

Personal logos for the world's top tennis players are something of a recent phenomenon. Federer's is perhaps the most recognisable – a subtle monogram of his two initials, very understated and classy, just like the player himself. It's most effective when you see it on the blazer he often wears on top of his tennis kit when striding confidently onto court.

Djokovic's logo is more convoluted. A mash-up of alpha (the first letter in the Greek alphabet), medieval Serbian initials, and a symbol of a flying bird, it somehow combines to create his initials.

Andy Murray's logo, meanwhile, combines his initials with the number 77, a reference to his management company and the fact that, in 2013, he became the first male Briton in 77 years to win the Wimbledon singles title.

Of these four logos, Rafa's is the only one that doesn't feature his initials. But it certainly conveys the dynamism and power that he brings to his game.

Rafa's rapidly expanding business empire, coupled with his sporting success on a global scale, has led the player himself to admit his family has a certain Mafioso image – certainly to outsiders. "There is something Sicilian about the closeness of the Nadal family circle," John Carlin wrote in *Rafa: My Story*. "They live on a Mediterranean island, and more than a family, they are a clan – the Corleones, or the Sopranos, without the malice, or the guns. They communicate in a dialect only the islanders speak; they are blindly loyal to one another, and they conduct all business within the family."

Sebastián has often boasted that, when it comes to the Nadals, family loyalty is far more important than money. Perhaps so. But that's easy to say when there are such vast amounts of money swilling around the clan.

All this wealth naturally commands a sizeable tax bill. Unlike many of his tennis-playing peers, Rafa has never been lured away to a tax haven. Among his peers he really is something of an anomaly in this regard. When this book was written, the lion's share of his peers in the top 25 of the ATP world rankings had relocated to territories with no, or very low, income tax. The following had opted for Monaco, which levies no income tax at all: Novak Djokovic, Daniil Medvedev, Stefanos Tsitsipas, Alexander Zverev, Matteo Berrettini, Hubert Hurkacz, Felix Auger-Aliassime, Jannik Sinner and Grigor Dimitrov. Denis Shapovalov chose the

BELOW: At a charity match in Cape Town, South Africa, in 2020.

Bahamas, Gael Monfils was in Switzerland, and Dan Evans in Dubai, all avoiding the more punitive tax regimes of their home nations.

In Spain, the current top rate of personal income tax is 47 per cent which Rafa happily pays, albeit with perhaps slightly gritted teeth. "I'm Spanish, and I'm happy to be," he said in a recent interview in an Italian newspaper. "Of course, when the tax bill arrives, I'm a little less happy. But I had the good fortune to be born in a country of many virtues, which gave me a good life."

In 2017 he explained his tax status in more detail. "In terms of managing assets, perhaps it would be better to go to another country with more beneficial conditions, but Spain is where I'm happy, with my family and friends. In another country, I would have double the money but be only half as happy. Money doesn't buy happiness."

ABOVE: Rafa's car sponsor Kia regularly gifts him new sets of wheels.

Rafa knows he would be miserable if he lived elsewhere, away from his beloved Mallorca, his loyal family and friends. Relocation to a tax haven might save him millions in income tax, but his state of mind would suffer, and consequently so would his tennis. In the end, it would be a false economy.

"Federer versus Nadal embodies righty versus lefty. Classic technique versus ultramodern. Feline light versus taurine heavy. Middle European restraint and quiet meticulousness versus Iberian bravado and passion. Dignified power versus an unapologetic, whoomphing brutality. Zeus versus Hercules. Relentless genius versus unbending will. Polish versus grit. Metrosexuality versus hypermuscular hypermasculinity. A multi-tongued citizen of the world versus an unabashedly provincial homebody. A private-jet flier versus a steerage passenger. A Mercedes driver versus a Kia driver."

From *Strokes of Genius* by L. Jon Wertheim

THE MATCH

WIMBLEDON

July 6th 2008
All England Club, London, UK
Final: Rafa Nadal vs. Roger Federer
Rafa Nadal beat Roger Federer 6–4, 6–4, 6–7, 6–7, 9–7

The wounds were still raw from his loss to Roger Federer in the Wimbledon final the year before. So when Rafa returned to the All England Club in the summer of 2008, this time he was determined he would end the day as champion.

Although he had already beaten Federer three times that year, all the victories had been on clay. As always, when it came to grass, the Swiss player's style of tennis lent him a distinct advantage. But, in the run-up to the clash, what no one could fathom was which man might win the psychological battle of minds that day. In tennis matches at this level, it is often the mind that is the greatest weapon.

Rafa's final hours of preparation for that fateful match were little different from usual. On a drizzly south London Sunday morning, he arrived at the All England Club at 10.30am for a warm-up on the club's practice courts with his agent Carlos Costa, which was cut short by rain. After a simple lunch of pasta with just olive oil and salt, plus a small piece of fish, he then made his way to the locker-room for a freezing-cold shower – a ritual he says energises him. He needed a painkilling injection in his foot, because of an injury he had been carrying. Sitting in front of his locker, number 101, he then wrapped new grips onto his rackets, before asking his physical therapist to strap up his aching knees. Federer was also in the locker room, only a few paces away at locker number 66.

Rain caused a short delay to the championship final itself but, finally, both players made the long, nervous walk down corridors and stairs to Centre Court, welcomed enthusiastically and noisily by the capacity crowd waiting there.

The style and comportment of each player could hardly have been different. Both may have been sponsored by Nike, but their kit was starkly contrasting. Federer, ever the gentleman, wore a classic woollen cardigan emblazoned on the left breast with his famous RF monogram. Underneath was an equally classic polo shirt. Rafa sported a zip-up tracksuit, below which was a tight, sleeveless vest, and his knee-length shorts. One item they both wore was a thick, white headband. While Federer's hair flopped nonchalantly over the top of his headband, Rafa's longer locks were tied back securely.

Federer had won the toss and elected to serve. At 2.35pm, 35 minutes after the official match start time, the Swiss reigning champion tossed the first yellow Slazenger ball into the air and struck it hard. It clipped the top of the net for a let serve. Replaying the first serve, Federer's confident stroke looked to be a winner but Rafa just managed to return it. Then, most unusually for the first point of a Grand Slam final, there followed a 14-stroke rally that Rafa eventually won with a deep forehand to the far left-hand corner, beyond Federer's reach. It was just one point of the 412 that were to follow, but it was a portent of the epic match ahead.

What followed is considered by many tennis experts, to not only be the greatest Wimbledon final in the 144-year history of this tournament, but the greatest tennis match of all time.

BELOW: Although they are both sponsored by Nike, the styles of the two players couldn't have been more contrasting.

Like all the best matches, it see-sawed back and forth, teasing the spectators – and stretching the two opponents – again and again with hints as to who might triumph overall.

Rafa later revealed that he'd embarked on the match with a very simple strategy: keep pressurising Federer's backhand, hoping to "wear him down, break that easy rhythm of his, frustrate him, drive him close to despair".

It was a strategy that, during the initial two sets at least, worked bountifully. The first he won 6–4, in 48 minutes; the second by the same margin, despite being four games to one down at one point. Part of the Mallorcan's tactics included a glacially slow service routine. Post-match analysis showed that, thanks to all his tics and rituals, the average time he took to complete each service was 30 seconds. Unbearably for Federer, in that second set, many of those serves took even longer than that. The umpire Pascal Maria eventually lost patience and imposed a time violation on Rafa.

To turn things around, the defending champion needed a bit of rhythm-breaking of his own. It appeared to come in the third game of the third set when Rafa slipped awkwardly on changing direction. Fortunately the trainer, Michael Novotny, was able to treat his right knee and play resumed.

It was actually the weather that ended up breaking Rafa's rhythm. With black clouds looming, at 5–4 to Federer, the rain started to fall and the players were ushered off court. In a documentary released a decade later, Federer attributed this rain break to a switch in momentum, and the key to dislodging a certain lethargy that had crept in. "It took me two sets to shake it off and I believe that that rain delay probably woke me up. I said: 'If you're going to go out of this match, at least you're going to go down swinging.'"

When play resumed well over an hour later, it was Federer who gained the upper hand as the players ground on through to a tiebreak. With some blistering serves and forehands, the Swiss master punctuated that tiebreak with an ace to win it 7–5, and with it his first set of the match.

The next set followed a similar route, but this time the tiebreak was even more thrilling. Federer had to save two championship points before he clawed it back to level the match at two sets all. Many have compared that fourth-set tiebreak to the greatest tiebreak of all – the 1980 Wimbledon shoot-out between Bjorn Borg and John McEnroe.

At 7.53pm, with the fifth set balanced at two games all, deuce, the rain rudely interrupted proceedings again. Many feared the players would have to wait until the following day to conclude their battle. But half an hour later, with the daylight dwindling, they resumed play.

The denouement of the match will forever be remembered in sporting history. If the first rain break had helped Federer, the second was more beneficial to Rafa. At seven games all, crucially, he broke the mighty Swiss serve. Half the crowd were yelling "Roger! Roger!" at the top of their voices, the other half yelling "Rafa! Rafa!" In a final burst of energy it was the latter who took the championship – on his fourth championship point of the whole match – winning nine games to seven.

The ball was still rolling around at the bottom of the net, where Federer had inadvertently played it low, as Rafa dropped to the grass, falling flat on his back, like he always does, with his arms outstretched. At last, he had defeated his Wimbledon nemesis. After four hours and 48 minutes – at the time a record for the longest Wimbledon singles final – both players were physically and mentally exhausted. Many of the spectators, cheering hysterically, were mentally exhausted too. It was 9.16pm, and none of them had expected to be on Centre Court that late in the evening.

Nadal climbed, slowly and wearily, up to the players' box where his family and friends were waiting. They included both parents, uncles, aunts, friends, the professional golfer Gonzalo Fernandez-Castaño and the boss of Real Madrid football club. After hugging them, armed with a Spanish flag, he walked across the flat roof of the commentary booth to the royal box where his nation's Crown Prince Felipe and Princess Letizia were waiting to congratulate him too.

After the trophy ceremony, which was staged in a twilight illuminated by the flashes of thousands of cameras and mobile phones, it was in the post-match press conference that Rafa tried to sum up his emotions. "Impossible to describe, no? I don't know. Just very happy. It's unbelievable for me to have a title here in Wimbledon. It's probably, well, it's a dream. I always, when I was a kid, dreamt of playing here. But to win, it's amazing, no?"

The victorious Spaniard then quickly returned to his rental house, on Newstead Way, just a hundred yards or so west of the All England Club, to change into a dinner suit before hot-footing it to the champions' ball in the centre of town. It was 4am the following day before he got back home to bed. When he slept, though, he enjoyed the sleep of a first-time Wimbledon champion.

Rafael has the one thing that Roger doesn't: balls. I don't even think Rafael has two; I think he has three.

Mats Wilander

**RAGING
BULL**

Of all the leading players currently plying their trade on the ATP tour, Rafa has one of the most distinctive, aggressive and physically intimidating playing styles. Here we break down each element, analysing what makes it so effective.

Forehand

The grip Rafa uses on his forehand is what's known as a semi-western grip, so that the face of the racket is slanted towards the ground when he brushes up through the ball. The racket head starts in front of his body, and then moves past the left side of his face before swinging far behind him, low to the ground. In order to impart such heavy topspin, he uses his whole body like a massive whip, uncoiling each segment – leg, buttocks, midriff, shoulder, arm, wrist – in turn so as to increase the revolutions per minute (RPM) on the ball. The racket head comes forward, across the front of his body, strikes the ball – with his whole torso opened up at this stage – and then follows all the way round the back of his body, finishing up by his left shoulder.

The more infamous version of his forehand – and one with a truly vicious amount of topspin – is what's know as the lasso, or buggy whip. Rafa and his coaches used to call it "the Nadalada". For this, the preparation is the same as above but the racket follow-through is much higher. In fact, after it strikes the ball, the racket swings upwards, over the top of and all the way round his head, skimming the top of his cranium, and finishing up with the racket head pointing directly behind him. It's a phenomenal shot to watch – almost as if he's wielding a lasso rope – and one that seems to twist his rotator cuff and elbow beyond what you would think was physically possible.

LEFT: Demonstrating his trademark lasso forehand at Roland Garros in 2021.

The precise number of RPM that he imparts on the tennis ball varies enormously with each shot. Some have estimated it at well over 3,000 RPM, others even more. It depends on factors such as the weather conditions, the court surface (he hits forehands flatter when he's not on clay, for example), how deeply into the court he wants to send the ball, and how much time he has to prepare for the shot.

One tennis coach has analysed this forehand in depth. San Francisco-based John Yandell used a high-speed camera to count the average number of revolutions on a tennis ball punished by Rafa's lasso forehand. "We measured one forehand Nadal hit at 4,900 RPMs," he said in an interview in the *New York Times*. "His average was 3,200 RPMs. Think about that for a second. It's a little frightening to contemplate.It takes a ball about a second to travel between the players' rackets. So a Nadal forehand would have turned over 80 times in the second it took to get to [his opponent's] racket."

The way Rafa manages to weaponise his forehand is stunningly effective, especially on clay. The extreme topspin means that he can hit the ball harder so that it travels faster but still loops down inside the baseline. Then, when the ball hits the court surface, the topspin makes it kick up sharply and suddenly. If opponents don't attack it instantly, the ball will bounce high over their heads. This means they have very little time to prepare for or execute their return shots.

Rafa describes it thus: "I try to put the ball deep and then it bounces up really high. It forces my opponent to go inside the court, but with risk. Or else he has to hit it three metres behind the baseline. So either on the defence, or a risky attack."

OPPOSITE AND BELOW: In extreme cases, Rafa's forehands have been measured to give the tennis ball as many as 4,900 revolutions per minute.

One of Rafa's hitting partners once described returning this forehand as "like you're breaking off your arm". In an interview in the *New York Times*, American coach Robert Lansdorp explained the efficacity of Rafa's lasso forehand: "He can do it from any place, almost to any ball, and make winners. He can hit it cross-court, down the line, wherever he wants to go. And he's probably done it since he was 10. Thank God nobody changed it and told him, 'Hey, that is not the way to hit a forehand'."

Backhand

Generally, Rafa prefers a topspin backhand. Using both hands – his right to guide the shot and his left to give it its energy – he starts with the racket in front of his body. Then he swings it right back behind his backside, almost horizontal with the ground, before bringing it forward at great speed to strike the ball in front of his body, driving the energy up through both legs. The follow-through, still two-handed, ends up all the way round the back of his body, almost as far as his right shoulder.

The sliced backhand is highly effective, too. Played with just the left hand, he uses it to change the pace of a rally, or to play an approach shot so that he can attack the net, or for one of his devastating dropshots.

ABOVE: Rafa displaying his backhand follow-through at Roland Garros in 2021.

Serve

In the early days, Rafa's serve was the weakest shot in his arsenal, often slow compared to his rivals. He admitted as much. Not surprising when you think of how he had to come to grips with his multi-handedness. But as his career has progressed, it has become more of a weapon, with aces and service winners much more common. His first serve – usually sliced, especially from the left-hand side, but sometimes a bit flatter – now regularly reaches speeds well above 120mph. During his entire playing career on the ATP tour, he has fired down over 3,780 aces – around 2,220 on hard courts, 950 on clay, and 600 on grass.

His second serve, either topspin or slice, is slower and safer. An ATP study from 2019 measured it at an average of 96.4mph, just ahead of Djokovic's and Federer's. Interestingly, in the same study, Rafa's second serve had a winning percentage higher than any other player in that year's world top ten ranking – again just ahead of Djokovic and Federer.

As a left-hander, Rafa's serve is particularly effective when played to a right-hander in the advantage court (the right-hand court as he looks at it) since it swings out wide, far beyond the tramlines, pulling the opponent out of position. Should he place heavy topspin on it, this ensures it kicks up high, making it even more tricky for a right-hander to return. Federer has struggled for many years with this aspect of Rafa's serve.

In preparation for his serve, Rafa uses a stance called the pinpoint stance, where his back foot moves closer to his front foot as he takes the racket back behind his back.

Former Roland Garros finalist Alex Corretja recently analysed Rafa's serve, explaining how it differs from the one he used earlier in his career. Crucially, Rafa doesn't bend his knees as much as he used to when launching into the service action, adopting a more erect stance. This allows him to get back into the ready position very quickly after the serve, in preparation for the following shot. He also takes the racket higher on his serve, opening up his wrist when striking the ball, and giving the serves more speed.

The ATP tour's Craig O'Shannessy has analysed Rafa's serve in great detail. Here are some of his findings from the 2019 season: at the start of the service game, most first serves (62%) are sliced down the T, while 25% are sent wide, and just 13% to the opponent's body. "The thinking here is to start the game on the right foot with what he knows best, and surge to 15–love as many times as possible," O'Shannessy says.

At 15–all, it's a similar story, with 51% of first serves down the T, 36% wide and 13% at the body. If he finds himself 30–love up, however, he allows himself a little breathing room, and he can afford to be a bit more creative, sending the majority of his serves (52%) out wide, with 42% going down the T and just 6% to his opponent's body. On the other hand, if he finds himself 30–love down, he has to be more cautious, sending 49% wide, 37% down the T and 15% to the body.

Physical and mental game

Rafa essentially wins by grinding down his opponents and waiting for the correct moment to kill the point. "My game is to play with the rallies," he once explained. "I don't want to play serve-and-volley, or serve and one shot, or ace. Everybody has to know that. My game is to play with intensity, play good rhythm all the time, and try to play a long time without having mistakes."

To make this attritional form of tennis work, he needs incredible footwork and tactical court coverage, something he has turned into an art form that is often mesmerising to watch.

But the physical game is nothing without the mental strength to back it up. Djokovic has been very complimentary about this combination in his rival. "Rafael is the physically strongest player on he tour," he once said, "and mentally he has this unbelievable ability to stay focused from the first to the last point of the match, whether he's playing in the Wimbledon final or in the first round of a minor tournament."

Former French Davis Cup captain Guy Forget explained it even better. "Nadal really is a brutal force. He possesses the mental strength for anything. Even when he's in trouble, when he has blisters on his feet, he manages to dominate. He's a monster in defence. You think you've won the point; he's back in the sponsor's hoarding, five metres behind the baseline, and then he pulls off a passing shot, and everyone wonders how he did it."

LEFT: Fast court coverage at Roland Garros in 2019.

RIGHT: Rapid reactions at Roland Garros in 2017.

"Some people get very confused about my game. They think it's better if the court is slow, because I have a good defence. But the faster it is, the better for me. My spin is more painful for my opponents, my aggressive game works better.

Rafa Nadal

The grunting

Rafa's certainly not the first player to grunt loudly when he strikes the ball. Nor will he be the last. From Jimmy Connors back in the 1970s, through to Monica Seles in the 1990s and, more recently, the Williams sisters, Maria Sharapova, Victoria Azarenka (or 'Vika the shrieker'), Andy Murray and Novak Djokovic, many players have filled tennis stadia with the sound of loud grunting or shrieking. Rafa's are more quiet than many other players'.

But he'd be wise not to alter the habit. Experts suggest that grunting as one strikes the ball adds a small percentage of extra power to each shot. It gives players extra assertion on court. Famed American coach Nick Bollettieri claimed that grunting gives players a "psychological and physiological release of tension". There are other benefits. When one player hits the ball, the opponent simultaneously uses the sound of that ball on the racket to gauge the speed and depth of shot coming towards him. Grunting disguises this sound, therefore placing the opponent at a slight disadvantage.

Rafa's racket

Rafa has been wielding Babolat tennis rackets since he was eight years old. Over the years, he has fine-tuned the various models. As a youngster he preferred the lighter Soft Drive model, later graduating to the Pure Drive. Then in 2004 he started using the new Aero model. "It was engineered specifically for spin," the company claims. "Featuring an aerodynamic section to increase head speed which gave the ball more rotations per minute, it proved perfect for the topspin-heavy game with which Nadal was about to conquer the tennis world."

The racket strings play a crucial role in Rafa's topspin game, too. Although at times during his career he has flirted with Luxilon Big Banger strings, in late 2009 he started using an octagonal (rather than the more usual cylindrical) string, called the Babolat RPM Blast. "Sheathed in silicon, it grabs the ball for better lift and spin," the manufacturers explain. "When Rafa agreed to test the RPM Blast, everyone held their breath. After about 15 minutes, he announced the verdict: 'not bad'. Then, just a few days later, his coach Toni Nadal left a message for the competition department: 'The string is very good indeed. We need more!'"

In 2011, as he started positioning himself further up the court for his groundstrokes – closer to the baseline than he used to play – he asked Babolat to add extra weight to the top of the racket head in order to create more head speed on his shots. "Babolat's customisation team worked on the addition of a sliver of weight tape at the top of his frame to increase the powerful hammer effect," Babolat explain. "That added three grams to the weight – in relative terms a big increase." In 2016 a further two grams of tape were added to the top of the frame.

The latest incarnation of Rafa's Aero is called the Babolat Pure Aero RAFA. Guillaume Cambon is one of the technicians who works for Babolat on the frame. "Apart from these strips of weight tape at the top of the frame, there is almost no specific customisation of his racket,' he claims. Jean-Christophe Verborg is Babolat's director of competition. He says his client is supplied with a batch of between six and eight new rackets four times a year.

It's important to state that virtually none of the higher-ranked professional players use the same model of racket that is sold to the public. Nearly all of them customise them in some way. No serious elite player would dream of buying a new racket online or from a sporting goods shop and stepping straight out onto court with it. Like racing cars, every aspect needs to be fine-tuned to perfection. Some players have even been known to use a different brand of racket underneath their sponsor's paint job. (There's no suggestion that Rafa does this, however.)

The strings are the first area to receive attention. In virtually every country around the world (except the UK, for some bizarre reason) rackets are sold unstrung so that players can choose their own stringing set-up. Among the top pros, this is a highly complicated business, requiring experienced racket stringers who thread their player's rackets with strings in a specific material, gauge, pattern and tension.

Most players also use strips of lead to alter the weight, balance and head speed of their rackets, sticking it to the frame, like Rafa. Some even open up the butt cap at the base of the racket handle and insert extra weight inside in the form of lead, silicone or epoxy.

The handle itself is often different to the handle you'll see on rackets in the shops. Many pros are so meticulous in their demands that they ask their racket technicians to change the ratio of the bevels on the handle, for example, or even the length of the handle in some cases.

So what exactly is the weapon that Rafa goes into battle with? It depends who you believe. Babolat insist he uses the Babolat Pure Aero RAFA. But most experts suggest he actually plays with a heavier and less forgiving model called the Babolat AeroPro Drive Original.

Jonathan Hudson is editor of online tennis magazine perfect-tennis.com. According to his analysis, Rafa's current model is 27 inches long, with a head size of 100 square inches, a strung weight of 343 grams (lighter than both Federer's and Djokovic's), a stringing pattern of 16x19, a grip size of 4.25 inches (otherwise known as L2), covered by a Babolat Syntec Pro Black grip and a Babolat VS original white overgrip.

Rafa's choice of grip size is fairly small, especially when you consider that he doesn't have small hands. But the player himself claims this allows him to generate more topspin. "I like the small grip because I have better control of what I am doing with the hand," he said in an interview with *GQ* magazine. "I can produce more spins than when I have a bigger grip on my hand."

Hudson says the Babolat RPM Blast strings Rafa currently uses have a 15L gauge/1.35mm, usually strung at a tension of 55 pounds per square inch. "At the start of 2016, Nadal briefly switched to Luxilon Big Banger Original 130 strings to obtain more power," he adds. "While the string did provide more power, Nadal felt he had less control due to the strings moving more (becoming more spaced out), and it didn't take long for him to move back to the Babolat RPM Blast setup."

Interestingly, you'll never see Rafa throw or smash his racket in frustration. "Because as a child I was taught that it is not done," he once explained. "It is I who am wrong, not the racket."

Jaume Pujol-Galceran and Manel Serras, Spanish authors of the book *Rafael Nadal: Master on Clay*, have analysed Rafa's self-discipline. "Nadal has never smashed his racket on the ground in anger," they write. "He never utters a word out of place, and never directs a tactless gesture towards his opponents. He always shows respect on the court. Granted, he jumps, gesticulates, brandishes his fist more than a few times, but never to taunt the player opposite, only to connect with his family and friends. Toni taught him to congratulate his adversary courteously after every match, whatever the result. It was a correctness he never lost while playing on the tour."

Rafa's support team

For 27 years they were one of the most famous double acts in tennis. Rafa and Uncle Toni. Living in and out of each other's pockets, what would one be without the other?

But their relationship eventually became something of a love-hate affair. Rafa always expressed a deep respect for his uncle, bordering on adoration. As a youngster, he believed Toni was imbued with superhuman powers. Toni told young Rafa that he had won the Tour de France, had played centre forward for AC Milan and that he had the supernatural ability to make it rain at will. Rafa nicknamed his uncle "Mago", or Magician.

At the same time, though, Rafa often described his uncle as "grumpy" and "quarrelsome". Some of Toni's coaching tactics bordered on the cruel. For example, uncle and nephew would play matches where the winner was the first to win 20 points. Toni would let Rafa get to 19, before stepping up a gear and blasting him off the court, 20 points to 19.

Toni, who played national rather than international level tennis as a younger man, had strong views on how children ought to be raised, refusing to indulge them in any way.

Toni stopped coaching Rafa in 2017. The story of how these two supposed inseparables finally parted company is a very odd one. Italian journalist Lorenzo Cazzaniga was with Toni when the coach announced, out of the blue, his decision to cease working with his nephew.

BELOW LEFT: Rafa and his Uncle Toni worked together as player and coach for 27 years – an inseparable duo.

BELOW RIGHT: Toni carries Rafa's trophy at Roland Garros in 2017.

"I was in Budapest, in February 2017, interviewing a South Korean tennis player," Cazzaniga remembers. "It just happened that Toni Nadal was also in Budapest for a tennis coaches' conference, so I took the opportunity to interview him as well."

At one point during their conversation, Toni dropped a bombshell. He told Cazzaniga that, the following year, he would stop coaching Rafa and start working at the Nadal Tennis Academy.

"I said, 'Wait! You know we are recording this conversation?'" Cazzaniga remembers. "Toni said, 'Yes, I know', as if splitting up with his nephew after 27 years was the most ordinary thing in the world. I checked three times with him that he wanted everyone to know this, and he confirmed that he did."

Understandably, Cazzaniga assumed Rafa was already well aware of Toni's decision, so he published the story straight away on his website TennisItaliano.it. Here is a translation of Toni's words from that interview:

"Rafa and I never had anything to argue about. But until he was 17, I decided everything. Then the agent Carlos Costa came along, his father got closer to him, and everybody had their own opinion. And the truth is that, with every passing year, I get to decide less and less, until there comes a point where I won't get to decide anything any more."

The following day the world's press were all over the story. There were prominent articles in the *New York Times*, *El Pais*, *L'Equipe* and other major newspapers and websites all over the planet.

But it turns out Rafa had no clue at all that his uncle was planning to sever the relationship. Suddenly Cazzaniga received a phone call from Rafa's communications chief, demanding to hear the original recording of the interview with Toni. Cazzaniga explained how he had assumed Rafa and Toni had already agreed on their split, and that he'd had no intention of dropping a bombshell like that.

Even now Cazzaniga still struggles to understand why Toni decided to tell him the news before alerting his nephew. "Maybe he believed Rafa wanted to split up the coaching partnership but felt he wasn't able to fire his uncle. After all, he had been with him since he was four years old. So, perhaps Toni took the decision to protect his nephew from having to make that decision himself. In essence, I think he made the split so Rafa didn't have to."

With Toni out of the picture, nowadays it is Carlos Moya who is Rafa's main coach. A fellow Mallorcan who he's practised with since turning pro, he was a highly talented player himself back in the 1990s and 2000s. In 1998 he won the French Open, and a year later he reached the coveted world number one spot.

As well as Roland Garros, he captured a further 19 singles titles on the ATP tour, including three Masters Series.

Rafa's assistant coach is Francis Roig, fulfilling a role he had for many years under Toni. Roig was a pretty handy player during the 1980s and 1990s, reaching a career high of number 23 in the world in doubles and 60 in the world in singles.

For many years, under the Toni regime, Carlos Costa was Rafa's agent, through the all-powerful global sports and entertainment agency IMG. Nowadays, Costa still represents Rafa, only as an independent agent instead, presumably saving the Nadal family a small fortune in agency fees.

Two other crucial members of the support team who have remained from the Toni days are his doctor Angel Ruiz Cotorro (who has been treating him since he was 14 years old) and his communications chief Benito Pérez Barbadillo ("irreverent, quick-witted, always cracking jokes"). There's also the physical trainer Joan Forcades, although Rafa calls on his services less and less as he reaches the end of his career.

There is one member of the team, however, who is perhaps more important than all the others put together, and that's Rafa's physical therapist Rafael Maymó, or Titín, as he's known. Maymó takes charge of more than just Rafa's physical side. You might describe him as an invaluable combination of physio, shrink, confidant, man Friday and shoulder to cry on. As Rafa winds down his career, it's not his playing technique and tactics that require the most attention. It's his physical and mental wellbeing. Maymó amply looks after both.

Cazzaniga describes Titín's role: "He is so important for Rafa's career. One of his best friends, he is the only person who has been at his side for his whole career and at all the tournaments. Sometimes Toni may not have been able to make it to a certain tournament; sometimes Carlos Moya couldn't make it. But Maymó is always there. He knows more about Rafa than anyone else. Even more than Toni does. When Rafa had a personal problem, he wouldn't go to Toni, he'd go to Maymó. Even when Rafa's father needed to ask something about Rafa, he went to Maymó instead of Toni. Maymó knows more about Rafa than even his wife does."

Rafa himself confirms this closeness between the two. "Take Titín away from my team and I'd be forlorn," he explained in his autobiography *Rafa: My Story*. "Were he to move on, filling the void of friendship he'd leave behind would be almost impossible. Not only is he a very good person, he is unfailingly honest. If he needs to say something to you, he'll tell it to you straight."

Rafa's fitness regime

Details of Rafa's training sessions on court and in the gym are closely guarded secrets. As the *Wall Street Journal* newspaper once explained: "Team Nadal sees no upside to revealing confidential information that could prove useful to his rivals."

However, it is clear that, over the years, Rafa has worked hard to bulk up his muscles in order to compete so aggressively on court. One only needs to look at his powerful figure to confirm this.

"When I was 16 or 17 years old, I worked with a pulley mechanism designed to help astronauts to combat atrophied muscles while in weightlessness," he once revealed. "I built up the muscles in my arms and my legs, especially my arms, in order to increase acceleration. This is the main reason I am able to impart more spin onto the ball with my topspin than any other player on the tour."

That topspin exacts a heavy toll on Rafa's left arm, especially the rotator cuff muscle in his left shoulder. For that reason, Rafa works hard to keep this particular part of his body functioning well.

He claims to do a lot less running training than other top male players, conscious that too much would add stress to his already suffering body. In the past, his fitness trainer has explained how most of the running he does involves sprint training in order to prepare for the explosive changes in speed and direction around the tennis court.

Training in the swimming pool, where the impact on his muscles and joints is lower, is also a favourite. A gym device called the BOSU board (or wobble board) helps with footwork and balance. There is always a huge amount of

ABOVE LEFT: Rafa's support team looks on at the Barcelona Open in 2014. In the top row (left to right) is Jordi 'Tuts' Robert from Nike, his father Sebastián and his manager Carlos Costa. In the bottom row (from left to right) is assistant coach Francis Roig, his physio Rafael Maymo and Uncle Toni.

ABOVE RIGHT: With Carlos Moya, in the old days, before the fellow Mallorcan became his coach.

stretching before and after each workout. Like many tennis players, Rafa uses ice baths after vigorous training sessions (and indeed matches) to reduce inflammation and prepare his body for the next round of abuse.

Rafa's injuries

Aggressive tennis exacts a heavy toll on a player's body. And Rafa has paid the price more than nearly all of his peers. (Opposite, you can see the whole back catalogue of his career injuries, in all its wincing glory.) His brutally physical, almost violent style of play – lunging, twisting, sprinting around the court, suddenly

TOP LEFT: With physical therapist, confidant and close friend Rafael Maymo at Roland Garros in 2021.

TOP RIGHT: Celebrating a winning shot in Canada in 2005.

LEFT: Warming up at Roland Garros in 2017.

INJURIES

Given the stress he puts his body through on court it's no surprise that injuries have frequently sidelined Rafa.

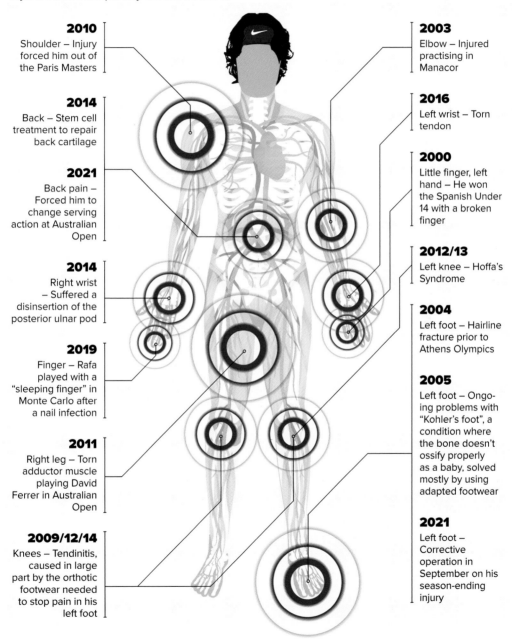

2010
Shoulder – Injury forced him out of the Paris Masters

2014
Back – Stem cell treatment to repair back cartilage

2021
Back pain – Forced him to change serving action at Australian Open

2014
Right wrist – Suffered a disinsertion of the posterior ulnar pod

2019
Finger – Rafa played with a "sleeping finger" in Monte Carlo after a nail infection

2011
Right leg – Torn adductor muscle playing David Ferrer in Australian Open

2009/12/14
Knees – Tendinitis, caused in large part by the orthotic footwear needed to stop pain in his left foot

2003
Elbow – Injured practising in Manacor

2016
Left wrist – Torn tendon

2000
Little finger, left hand – He won the Spanish Under 14 with a broken finger

2012/13
Left knee – Hoffa's Syndrome

2004
Left foot – Hairline fracture prior to Athens Olympics

2005
Left foot – Ongoing problems with "Kohler's foot", a condition where the bone doesn't ossify properly as a baby, solved mostly by using adapted footwear

2021
Left foot – Corrective operation in September on his season-ending injury

slamming on the brakes and changing directions – places an unbelievable amount of stress on his poor body. It's a wonder his career has survived this long.

Even back in the early 2000s, fellow player Andre Agassi warned of physical trouble to come. "Nadal is signing cheques that one can only hope his body will be able to pay," he said. "He plays hard for each point, and you can only hope he stays healthy, but there is a lot of wear and tear there. A great career depends not only on what he can do, but also on health."

All professional tennis players are destined to suffer from injuries at one time or another. The more industrious ones compete in up to 30 tournaments a year, battering, bruising and punishing their bodies week in week out. Granted, they can call upon the services of some of the best physiotherapists on the planet, but with such debilitating wear and tear, eventually something has to give.

For Rafa, his first major injury was in his left foot. It all started in 2004 when a stress fracture forced him to miss most of the clay-court season, including Roland Garros. The following year, the same foot flared up again. This time it was far more serious. Rafa's doctor Angel Cotorro wasn't able to give him a satisfactory diagnosis so he consulted a specialist in Madrid. It turns out Rafa was suffering from a congenital foot problem caused by a small bone in the foot (the tarsal scaphoid) which had failed to harden properly during his childhood. After all the years of tennis, the bone deformed, grew bigger, and risked splintering. Hence the extreme pain.

Rafa was then delivered the worst possible news: the specialist told him he might never play competitive tennis again. Rafa broke down and wept. He felt as though his life had been cut in half.

Fortunately, as ever, Rafa's family rallied round in support. Toni encouraged his nephew to keep on training, even though he was forced to hit balls while sitting in a chair or standing on crutches. Rafa's father remained optimistic they would find a solution.

Eventually, under guidance from the Madrid specialist, Rafa's shoe sponsors, Nike, succeeded in manufacturing a shoe with special cushioning on the sole to protect the damaged bone. To accommodate the new footwear, he had to tinker endlessly with his playing style, but, luckily, it eventually worked. There was still pain, but it was bearable. "We must equip ourselves to resist," he explained later. "Because there is no other solution than to resist."

The whole experience gave Rafa a new perspective on his career. Having come so close to losing his beloved profession, from then on he decided he would approach each and every match as if it were his last.

TOP LEFT: Rafa plays through a knee injury at Indian Wells in 2019.

TOP RIGHT: With his doctor Angel Ruiz Cotorro at Wimbledon in 2019.

BOTTOM LEFT: A foot injury takes its toll at the Australian Open in 2019.

BOTTOM RIGHT: The pain of an elbow injury at Wimbledon in 2010.

The left foot wasn't his only problem. There would be further injuries over the years: legs, shoulder, knees, wrist, hip, back, fingers. The adapted footwear actually made him more prone to knee injuries, but he needed that adapted tennis shoe to play.

The doping allegations

They called it Operación Puerto. Back in the mid-2000s, Spanish police launched an investigation into an alleged sports doping network involving several of the world's top cyclists and cycling teams. Amid all of the confusion, one European newspaper alleged that the doctor who was at the centre of the scandal, Eufemiano

Fuentes (who was later cleared of all charges), had a list of clients that included Rafa Nadal.

With not a shred of evidence provided against him, Rafa immediately protested his innocence and denied he was involved in doping in any way. Unfortunately, the seed of doubt was sown and, in subsequent years, other tennis players spread false rumours that he was guilty of taking performance-enhancing drugs. A high-profile French politician – Roselyne Bachelot, the country's minister for health and sports – went one step further. In 2016 she publicly accused him in a TV interview of doping. Rafa later sued her for defamation, claiming her comments were harmful to his image, and was awarded 12,000 euros, which he donated to charity.

"I intended not only to defend my integrity and my image as an athlete but also the values I have defended all my career," Rafa said after the court ruling. "I also wish to avoid any public figure from making insulting or false allegations against an athlete using the media, without any evidence or foundation and to go unpunished."

It's important to make one thing abundantly clear: there has never been a shred of evidence to suggest Rafa is guilty of doping. He has consistently protested his innocence. "I am a completely clean guy," he said in an interview in the Los Angeles Times. "I work so much during all my career, and when I get an injury, I get an injury. I never take nothing to be back quicker. And never had no temptation of doing something wrong. I believe in the sport and in the values of the sport. It is an example for the kids. If I am doing something that goes against that, I will be lying to myself, not to my opponents."

Testing for performance-enhancing drugs is managed by the International Tennis Federation, under their Tennis Anti-Doping Programme. It applies to all players at all elite levels of tennis, including the Grand Slams, the ATP tour, the WTA tour and the Olympics. Players are obliged to submit to urine or blood

> It's true that I went through some tough situations during all my career. But with the positive attitude and with the right people around – they were a key – I was able to find a way to keep going.

Rafa Nadal

testing at any time, in or out of competition, without advance notice. In addition, players ranked in the world top 100 must inform testers of their whereabouts every day of the year that they are not competing. Most years, only a handful of players are found to have committed doping violations.

During 2020 (the latest figures available as this book was being prepared), Rafa was tested a total of 12 times – four times during competition and eight times out of competition. This was less than usual, presumably because the global pandemic caused the cancellation of so many tournaments that year. In 2019, for example, he was tested 29 times; in 2018, 20 times. During his entire career he has never tested positive for any illegal substance. It's unfortunate – and many would say grossly unfair, given the complete lack of evidence – that Rafa's name has ever been linked to doping.

OLYMPIC RECORD

Rafa has won a gold medal in both singles and doubles. He is the most successful of the Grand Slam 20 Club: Roger Federer has won singles silver and Novak Djokovic bronze.

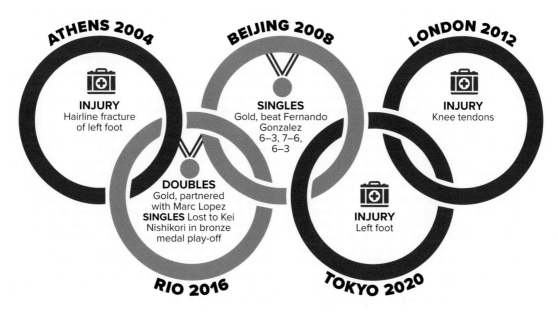

ATHENS 2004

INJURY
Hairline fracture
of left foot

BEIJING 2008

SINGLES
Gold, beat Fernando
Gonzalez
6–3, 7–6,
6–3

LONDON 2012

INJURY
Knee tendons

DOUBLES
Gold, partnered
with Marc Lopez
SINGLES Lost to Kei
Nishikori in bronze
medal play-off

INJURY
Left foot

RIO 2016

TOKYO 2020

THE MATCH

BEIJING OLYMPIC GAMES
August 17th 2008
Olympic Green Tennis Centre, Beijing, China
Final: Rafa Nadal vs. Fernando Gonzalez
Rafa Nadal beat Fernando Gonzalez 6–3, 7–6, 6–3

The Olympic Games rarely offers the very best quality of tennis. The rare occasions when it makes for truly exciting viewing is when players are attempting to capture what's known as the Golden Slam: all four Grand Slam singles titles, plus the Olympic singles gold medal in the same calendar year. Of course, this opportunity only comes around once every four years, giving it that extra-special cachet.

Rafa has never been in a position to take the Golden Slam. Only one player, Steffi Graf – has ever achieved that. In fact, Rafa hasn't managed to win all four Grand Slam singles titles in the same calendar year (known in the sport as "The Calendar Slam"). Not for want of trying, however; he came closest in 2010 when he won Roland Garros, Wimbledon and the US Open.

Nonetheless, his 2008 Olympic gold medal match deserves special mention, if only because it gave Rafa the points he required to finally break Federer's four-and-a-half-year reign at the world number one spot.

When second-seeded Rafa and his 12th-seeded Chilean rival Fernando Gonzalez found themselves either side of the net on the main court at Beijing's Olympic Green Tennis Centre on that hot August day in 2008, it was the latter who might have felt more confident. He had won both of the hard-court matches the duo had previously contested. Both players had managed an impressive run through the draw. With arguably the easier route to the final, Gonzalez didn't drop a set until the semi-finals where he was pushed to an 11–9 win in the deciding third set against American James Blake. Rafa, meanwhile, dropped a set in his nervous opening match, and another against Djokovic in the semi-finals.

Rafa, dressed in long white shorts, a dark-orange sleeveless top (with a tiny Spanish badge across the left breast), a light-orange headband, and supports across either knee, opened proceedings in his typical brutal style, firing his first serve down the T and then killing Gonzalez's subsequent return with a massive

forehand. The Chilean, in a more conservative black and white tennis kit, looked nervous. At the time he possessed one of the most devastating forehands in the world ... and occasionally he used it to great effect. But not enough on this particular day. And with Rafa, as all opponents know, you only need to reveal a tiny chink in your armour for him to rip it open mercilessly.

ABOVE: Only one other male player (Andre Agassi) has won Olympic singles gold plus all four Grand Slam singles titles.

In the first set, Rafa raced to a 3–0 lead, eventually winning 6–3. The most watchable set was the second, though, when Gonzalez manoeuvred himself into a double-set-point position with a beautiful, unreturnable inside-out forehand into the advantage service box. Having worked so hard to achieve this lead, though, he then squandered both set points; the first by pushing an easy volley wide, the second by dumping a forehand into the net.

These errors frayed his nerves further still so that he made three forehand errors in the ensuing tiebreak. The Spaniard eventually claimed it convincingly, 7–2.

From then on, Rafa was in dominant form, breaking serve to love in the fourth game, to move 3–1 up. Gonzalez fought bravely, and the squeaking of both players' shoes on the DecoTurf hard court grew increasingly loud. But all of Gonzalez's fighting was simply delaying the inevitable as his opponent then closed out the set 6–3 to take the match and the Olympic gold medal.

Later, at the medal ceremony, Rafa, in an ill-fitting Spain tracksuit, received his medal from fellow Spaniard Juan Antonio Samaranch. Gonzales obviously took

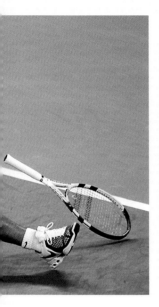

silver, while bronze went to Djokovic, who had beaten James Blake in the third-place play-off match. And yes, Rafa did bite his gold medal, just as he bites every trophy he wins. Finally he posed for the pack of photographers with the Spanish flag as his cape.

"I know how difficult it is to win these things, especially here, because you only have one chance every four years," he said in the press conference following the match. "In tennis, the Grand Slams are a little bit more important than here. But here you only have one chance every four years. The thing is, winning here, I feel like I won for all the country. That's more special, no? I win for a lot of people, not only for me."

Later he reassessed the importance of his win. "It's an honour to be part of the Olympic family of Spanish sport," he said. "What I lived through during the Olympic Games is something unforgettable, something you just can't find on the tour, even in a Grand Slam. That experience was one of the best of my life."

Perhaps the greatest aspect of Rafa's Olympic win was the way it later enabled him to complete what's known as the career Golden Slam: a gold medal plus victory in all four Grand Slams at any time in one's career. To this day, only two men – Rafa and Andre Agassi – have achieved this.

8

FAME IN SPAIN

s Rafael Nadal the most famous Spanish sportsperson of all time? There's no question he's the most famous Spanish tennis player. During the Open Era (the period from 1968, when tennis turned professional, until the present day), there have been just five world number-one-ranked singles players from Spain: Rafa, Carlos Moya (who is now Rafa's coach), Juan Carlos Ferrero, Arantxa Sánchez Vicario and Garbiñe Muguruza.

But, remember, there are world number ones, and there are world number ones. Rafa has spent a total of 209 weeks at the top spot (no other Spaniard comes anywhere close to this), and has 21 Grand Slam titles to his name so far. In comparison, Moya, Ferrero, Sánchez Vicario and Muguruza share just eight Grand Slam titles between the lot of them. (There is also one Spaniard from before the Open Era worthy of mention, and that's Manuel Santana who won Wimbledon, the US Open and two times at Roland Garros, all in the 1960s.)

What about other sports, though? Go back far enough in history and there are plenty of legendary bullfighters and pelota players from Spain, but given the nature of their sports, they faced little foreign competition. It wasn't until the death of the dictator General Franco (in 1975), Spain's subsequent path to democracy (in the early 1980s), and its accession to the European Union (in 1986) that the nation began truly to flex its sporting muscles. The economic prosperity that was built upon political stability allowed athletes – tennis players, golfers, footballers, basketballers, cyclists and racing drivers – to shine.

RIGHT: Receiving an award from Prince Felipe, the future king of Spain, in Madrid.

Perhaps the greatest catalyst of all was Spain's triumphant bid for the Olympic Games, which it staged in Barcelona in 1992. For Spaniards, and the rest of the world watching, that summer felt gloriously positive and upbeat as 169 nations and nearly 10,000 athletes congregated in the Catalan capital to compete. It was the first Summer Olympiad since the end of the Cold War, with several former Soviet and Yugoslavian republics competing under their newly independent flags. South Africa was invited after a 32-year ban. Germany sent a unified team for the first time since the 1960s. Riding the wave of all this positivity, and benefitting from their home advantage, Spanish athletes won a total of 22 medals, including 13 golds, placing them at sixth on the overall medal table.

Throughout the rest of that decade, the Spanish government constructed sports training facilities all over the country. The public and the media leapt on the bandwagon, fervently supporting their new sporting heroes. At grass-roots level, dozens of sports benefitted from government investment.

Suddenly the whole world started learning of new Spanish champions. In football we saw the likes of Cesc Fàbregas, Iker Casillas, David Villa, Sergio Ramos, Fernando Torres, Gerard Piqué, Xavi Hernández, Raúl González, Carles Puyol and Andrés Iniesta. Spain's national team won the World Cup in 2010 (and Rafa was in the dressing room to celebrate), and the Euros in 2008 and 2012.

RIGHT: With Spanish goalkeeper Iker Casillas and Princess Letizia (now Queen of Spain) after Spain won the World Cup in South Africa in 2010.

PREVIOUS PAGE: Leading the national delegation at the opening ceremony of the 2016 Rio Olympics.

IKER

Spaniards lit up golf courses, too, first with Seve Ballesteros and then with Sergio Garcia, José Mariá Olazábal (with whom Rafa has organised a charity golf tournament), Miguel Angel Jiménez and John Rahm garnering huge fan bases.

In Formula 1, Fernando Alonso won the world championship twice for Renault in 2005 and 2006 and came close to winning it for Ferrari. In MotoGP, Marc Marquez has won his championship six times. In road cycling, Miguel Indurain won the Tour de France five times.

Comparing the sporting achievements of a tennis player to a racing driver's, or a golfer's to a basketballer's, is an impossible task. You may as well stand in the middle of an orchard in Andalucia, in the midday heat, and compare oranges with lemons. How could you possibly line up tennis Grand Slams next to Formula 1 grand prix victories? How do weeks at number one in the ATP world rankings possibly compare with being crowned the champion club multiple times in La Liga?

Despite these obvious problems of sport metrics, Rafa still shines more brightly than all his compatriots, in all their sports, whichever way you measure his success: 21 Grand Slam singles titles; a further 69 ATP titles; two Olympic gold medals (one singles, one doubles); five Davis Cup team victories; 209 weeks ranked number one in the world; year-end world number one five times.

ABOVE: At a Real Madrid Champions League match in Madrid in 2010.

OVERLEAF: With Spanish golfer Sergio Garcia at a tournament in Castellon de la Plana in 2010.

THE 20 SLAMS CLUB

How does Rafa compare to the other members of the Big Three who have reached the 20 Grand Slam titles mark?

	Djokovic	Nadal	Federer
Age at Time of 20th Win	34 *(Wimbledon 2021)*	34 *(Roland Garros 2020)*	36 *(Australian Open 2018)*
Slams Played at 20th Win	65	60	72
Most Consecutive Finals	6	5	10
Most Consecutive Titles	4	3	3 (twice)
Slams Played at 1st Title	13	6	17
Win-Loss v Djokovic	-	10–7	6–11
Win-Loss v Nadal	7–10	-	4–10
Win-Loss v Federer	11–6	10–4	-

At time of 20th Grand Slam title

Grand Slam Breakdown: Titles (Wins/Matches)

	Djokovic	Nadal	Federer
Australian Open	9 (82)	2 (76)	6 (102)
French Open	2 (81)	13 (105)	1 (73)
Wimbledon	6 (79)	2 (53)	8 (105)
US Open	3 (75)	4 (64)	5 (89)

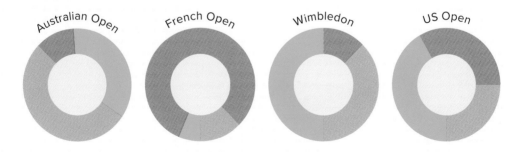

Australian Open   French Open   Wimbledon   US Open

LEFT: A trio of Spanish World No.1 tennis players: Carlos Moya, Juan Carlos Ferrero and Rafael Nadal in non-branded apparel at the Imperial Ancestral Temple, Beijing, 2005. They were promoting the China Open tournament.

In 2020, Spain's leading sports newspaper, *Marca*, asked its readers to vote for their nation's greatest of all time, or GOAT. "The Spanish GOAT battle," is how they presented their knock-out poll of 16 legendary Spanish athletes (most of them mentioned above). The winner, by a vast margin, was of course Rafa.

"Spain has had no shortage of sporting glory in recent years, making it an almost impossible task to choose the standout star," they wrote. "However, after a battle to find the country's sporting GOAT, Rafa Nadal has taken the prize."

In a recent interview, fellow Spanish tennis player Alex Corretja summed up his colleague's success rather neatly. "When Rafael Nadal wins, we all win," he told the sports website sport.es after Rafa secured his 20th Grand Slam title in 2020. "It is very difficult for me to summarise what Rafa means for all of us. For me, he is the best Spanish athlete of all time, with absolute respect for everyone else. I want to remember that Rafa is human, even though he acts like a machine; that he is sensitive, even if he looks like iron; and that his game can be as overwhelming as lava from a volcano."

ALL-TIME NUMBER OF MATCHES WON

In terms of all-time wins on the ATP tour, Rafa is very close to the summit.*

* After 2022 Australian Open

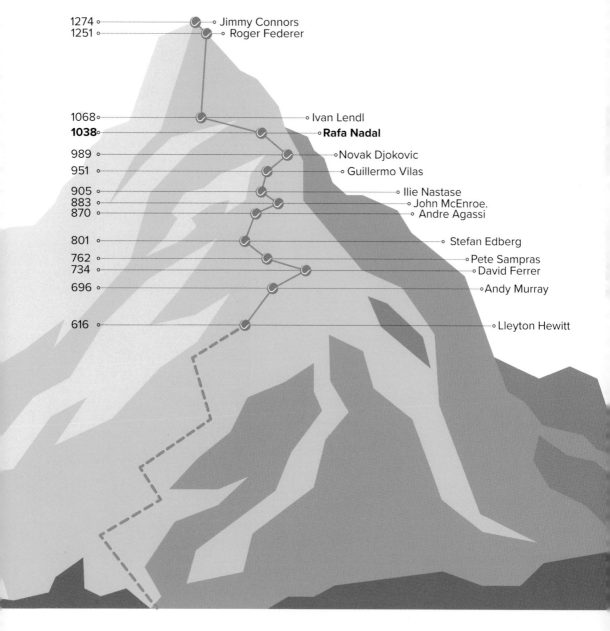

1274 — Jimmy Connors
1251 — Roger Federer

1068 — Ivan Lendl
1038 — **Rafa Nadal**
989 — Novak Djokovic
951 — Guillermo Vilas

905 — Ilie Nastase
883 — John McEnroe.
870 — Andre Agassi

801 — Stefan Edberg

762 — Pete Sampras
734 — David Ferrer

696 — Andy Murray

616 — Lleyton Hewitt

> I respect Rafa, probably more than any other player in the world; he is the biggest rival I had in my life. Everything he has achieved, his dedication to tennis and the way he goes about practising and tennis in general, these traits of his are worthy of admiration.

Novak Djokovic

THE MATCH

US OPEN
September 13th 2010
Billie Jean King National Tennis Center, New York City, USA
Final: Rafa Nadal vs. Novak Djokovic
Rafa Nadal beat Novak Djokovic 6–4, 5–7, 6–4, 6–2

The 2010 season was surely Rafa's greatest of all. That year he was triumphant at the French Open, Wimbledon and the US Open, becoming the first male player in tennis history to win Grand Slam singles titles on clay, grass and hard courts in the same year.

Arriving at the USTA Billie Jean King National Tennis Center in New York that year, Rafa, the world number one, was bristling with energy and confidence. All the way through to the final he hadn't dropped a single set. Djokovic, on the other hand, was forced to battle through a brutal five-set match in the first round against Viktor Troicki that dragged on for three hours and 40 minutes. In the semi-finals, against Roger Federer, he was kept working for even longer, in another tough five-setter that drained his energy reserves. Nevertheless, the Serb was determined to put on a strong fight against Rafa. Indeed, at times it felt more like heavyweight boxing than tennis.

While the players often performed at the highest level, the tournament's TV partners CBS let themselves down. With the final already postponed from the Sunday to the Monday, and knowing there was another storm rolling up the eastern seaboard, they nevertheless insisted on a late start to the match in order to hit the early-evening viewing schedule and the commercial opportunities that offered. Had they opted to stage the match earlier, it might all have been over before the rain arrived.

The two rivals – Rafa dressed all in black, with luminous yellow shoes, and Djokovic in white shirt and black shorts – embarked on their match with total energy, requiring over half an hour to complete the first five games. The opening point itself was something of a marathon, contested over 19 shots. The rally at 30–all in the second game was even longer, stretching to 28 strokes. By the time the players reached the fifth game of what was obviously going to be a mighty slug-fest, Djokovic was forced to defend no fewer than six break points. Rafa let five of those slip before slamming a massive forehand winner. He then went on quickly to take the first set.

The Serb upped the ante in the second set, racing to a 4–1 lead, the metronomic exchange of their grunting and the squeaking of their shoes giving longer rallies a strangely hypnotic feel. But Rafa fought back hard, levelling at four games all, 30–all. It was then that the storm arrived, forcing a delay of nearly two hours.

ABOVE: The 2010 US Open was Rafa's ninth Grand Slam singles title.

On their return, both players seemed even more fired up, playing with greater intensity. It was the Serb who closed out that second set.

If Rafa was demoralised by this, he certainly didn't show it. Some astoundingly intense play awarded him the third set. In the third game of the fourth set he broke Djokovic's serve, before galloping through to overall triumph. After three hours and 43 minutes, Djokovic sent his last forehand wide. Nadal dropped to the floor on his back, before rolling round onto his front, head in hands, like a man who had taken a bullet. His emotion spilled over, his back heaving up and down as he sobbed for joy.

Afterwards, he was asked to analyse his greatest strengths as a player. "The mentality, attitude on court I think always was good for me," he said. "I am positive on court, and I fight all the time. When I am playing well, the intensity always is high. The rhythm is high. I can play at the same rhythm and the same level [for a] long time."

Djokovic was gracious towards the victor. "It's great for somebody who had so much success as he did, [at a] very young age, to be able to continue motivating himself to perform his best at each tournament; each match he plays, regardless who he has across the net. You just have to put a hat down for this guy. Everything he does on and off the court. Great champion, great person, and great example of an athlete."

But it was perhaps the famous American coach Brad Gilbert who summed up Rafa's performance that night most succinctly. "Rafa's fortitude is just off the charts," he said. "He just doesn't give up, whether or not it's 40–love up or 40–love down. He just doesn't take a point off."

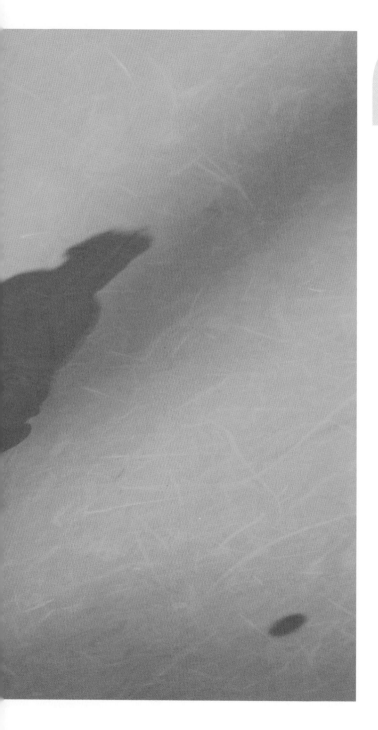

"For the first time in my career, I played a very, very good match in this tournament. That's my feeling, no? I played my best match in the US Open at the most important moment.

Rafa Nadal, after the 2010 US Open

FAMILY

In a nation, and on an island, where family members are often inseparable, Rafa and his family are more inseparable than most. Close-knit would be an understatement. The relationship between this tennis player, his parents, grandparents, aunts, uncles, nephews, nieces and cousins – many of whom he has spent much of his life living cheek-by-jowl with – is incredibly intimate. Financially, emotionally, psychologically and culturally, they almost operate as a single entity.

If you believe Rafa himself, for most of his existence, this family life has been happy, stable, united, harmonious, reassuringly familiar. When Rafa is content, all his extended family is content. When he is sad, all are sad. As described in Chapter 6, the Nadals are like a mafia but "without the malice, or the guns".

So when, in 2009, his parents Sebastián and Ana Maria announced that, after nearly 30 years of marriage, they were planning to divorce, for Rafa, especially, the news was a devastating blow.

It was his father who first told him he and his mother were separating. He relayed the news to his son on the flight home after his victory over Federer at the Australian Open. "Suddenly, and utterly without warning, the happy family portrait had cracked," he explained in his biography *Rafa: My Story*. "The continuity I so valued in my life had been cut in half, and the emotional order I depend on had been dealt a shocking blow."

LEFT: Team Nadal at the US Open in 2016. Top row from left to right: his mother Ana Maria, his wife Mery, sister Maribel. Middle row: father Seabstián (red shirt). Bottom row: Uncle Toni (green shirt) and his agent Carlos Costa (blue shirt).

Initially, the effect on Rafa's tennis seemed insignificant. That spring, he won the Masters Series tournaments in Indian Wells, Monte Carlo and Rome. But come Roland Garros, the cracks in his brave face had started to appear. He lost in the fourth round in Paris against Swedish player Robin Soderling. It is still one of only four defeats he has ever suffered at the French Open. As the season progressed, his dominance waned, and a knee injury flared up, exacerbated, he said, by the disintegration of his parents' relationship back home. He didn't even make it to Wimbledon that year. Then, to make matters worse, during the North American hard-court swing, he tore an abdominal muscle. By August that year he had dropped from number one in the world to number three. Granted, not a total disaster in the grand scheme of things, but an indication of how parental turmoil was affecting both his mind and his body.

"My parents' divorce made an important change in my life," he later explained. "It affected me. After that, when I can't play Wimbledon, it was tough. For one month I was outside the world."

Fortunately, the rest of his family rallied round in support. By the end of 2009 he realised he needed to shake himself out of his torpor. After specialist treatment on the knee injury (see Chapter 7), he began to turn his fortunes around.

In 2010 there was victory at Roland Garros (revenge over Soderling), his second Wimbledon title, and his maiden win at the US Open. Yes, Rafa was back; Rafa was back with a vengeance.

LEFT: Celebrating at the Madrid Open in 2009.

RIGHT: After the separation of his parents, Rafa lost to Soderling at the 2009 French Open. His misery is obvious.

LEFT: Winning the
2010 US Open.

Two years later there were rumours that Sebastián and Ana Maria had rekindled their relationship. Few outside the family group are sure whether this is actually true. It's more likely they have simply agreed to bury their differences and attend Rafa's tournaments together, as they used to in the old days, in an effort to bring back some stability to their son's tennis career.

There's no doubt his support team and his family provided a vital crutch during all this turmoil. His sister Maribel, especially, was a solace.

While Rafa was spending his educational years on the tennis court with Uncle Toni, Maribel was busy developing her own career as a businesswoman. As a child she studied at the Colegio Pureza de María, a renowned Catholic school in the family's home town. It was here that she made friends with Maria Francisca Perelló, or Mery, the girl she would introduce to her brother, and whom he would eventually marry. After school, Maribel studied sports science and sports management in Barcelona, and business management in Palma de Mallorca. Later she worked for the likes of sports and entertainment agency IMG (who once represented her brother), insurance company Mapfre (one of her brother's sponsors) and Banco Santander (another of her brother's sponsors). Nowadays she is essentially employed by her brother, working in marketing for the Rafa Nadal Academy. This may all sound rather nepotistic, but it's further proof of the Nadal family's close-knit business.

RIGHT: Rafa's parents (shown here at Roland Garros in 2017) may no longer be married, but they are still friends.

Another of Rafa's employees is his wife Mery. Despite the fact she's married to one of the most famous sportsmen on the planet, not a great deal is known about her. An extremely private person, she virtually never agrees to be interviewed, a situation that has lent her an almost enigmatic, mythical personality. It is thanks to the unusual Mallorcan tradition of giving celebrities the space they need that her privacy has never been invaded. Had she and Rafa lived anywhere else in Europe, the tabloid press and the paparazzi would have hounded them constantly. It's another reason why the couple have never relocated from their island home.

On the very rare occasions Mery does give interviews, the questions are answered via email, revealing nothing personal. Even in Rafa's autobiography, she is quoted over just a few short lines, blandly explaining that she prefers not to travel with Rafa; that she eschews the world of public celebrity, finding it "asphyxiating".

Born Maria Francisca Perelló in 1988, also in Manacor, she is the only daughter of Bernat, who ran an estate agency, and María, who worked as a civil servant at Manacor's city council. A quick note on her name: the Spanish and international press have nicknamed her Xisca, although Rafa and his family call her Mery, or Mary – both spellings are used. "I have many names," she said in a recent interview with the Spanish version of *Vanity Fair* magazine. "People around me call me Mery. The first time they referred to me as Xisca was in the press. Nobody calls me that and it is the name I least identify with."

As a youngster, Rafa was very shy with girls. It took his sister to encourage the relationship between Mery and her brother. As far as anyone knows, she is the only serious girlfriend he has ever had.

LEFT: Wife Mery and sister Maribel at the Davis Cup in Madrid in 2019.

In October 2019, after 14 years as boyfriend and girlfriend, the two of them tied the knot at a wedding ceremony held at the Sa Fortalesa estate in Pollença, a town on the island's northern coast. Originally a 17th-century fort, built to defend Mallorca from pirates, the estate once featured in the BBC adaptation of John Le Carré's *The Night Manager*.

Ever modest, the Nadal family attempted to avoid too much pomp and ceremony of a celebrity wedding. Inviting the former Spanish monarchs, Juan Carlos I and Queen Sofía, did nothing to suppress the excitement, however. Others on the 200-strong guest list included fellow tennis players Feliciano López, Carlos Moya, David Ferrer, Juan Mónaco and their other halves.

TOP AND RIGHT:
Rafa and Mery tie the knot in Mallorca in 2019.

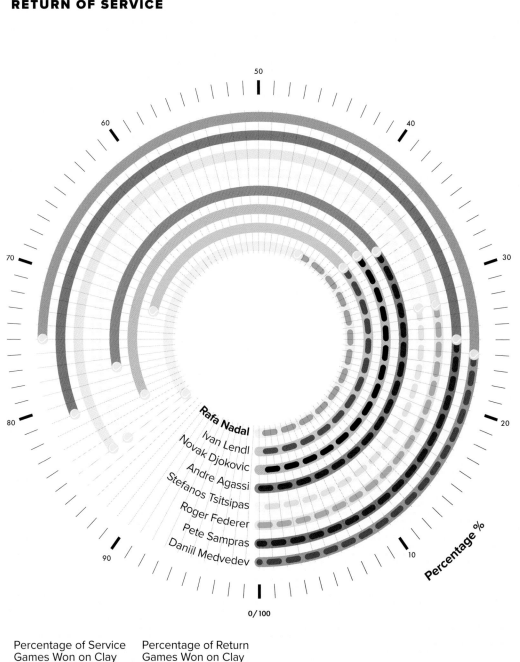

50
60
40
70
30
80
20
90
10

Rafa Nadal
Ivan Lendl
Novak Djokovic
Andre Agassi
Stefanos Tsitsipas
Roger Federer
Pete Sampras
Daniil Medvedev

Percentage %

0/100

Percentage of Service
Games Won on Clay

Percentage of Return
Games Won on Clay

A graduate in business management from the University of the Balearic Islands, Mery now works as director of her husband's children's charity, the Rafa Nadal Foundation. Her role involves travelling at least once a year to India, to the foundation's school (the Nadal Educational Tennis School) in Anantapur, in the south of the country. "I remember very well the impact it had on me the first time I was in Anantapur," she told *Vanity Fair*. "They live a reality so different from ours. Seeing what their expectations and priorities are in life is difficult to explain. I was shocked to see how the children at the school value the clothes and shoes that we give them. They keep them in their homes as if they were treasure."

Her charity work notwithstanding, Mery still keeps a very low profile. She rarely travels to her husband's tournaments – excepting the major moments in his career where she'll appear with Maribel and Ana Maria – at all times discreet and staying well out of the limelight.

And that's the way Rafa prefers it. "We've known each other forever, ever since we were little," he once explained. "Mery is my point of stability."

OPPOSITE: Rafa and Mery in Barcelona, in 2011.

THE MATCH

FRENCH OPEN

October 11th 2020

Stade Roland Garros, Paris, France

Rafa Nadal vs. Novak Djokovic

Rafa Nadal beat Novak Djokovic 6–0, 6–2, 7–5

Thirteen may be unlucky for most people, but not for Rafa at Roland Garros, in the autumn of 2020. Competing in a Covid-delayed French Open final, he demolished Novak Djokovic in three sets, requiring just two hours and 41 minutes to secure his 13th title at Roland Garros and his 20th Grand Slam overall.

In reality, the scoreline – 6–0, 6–2, 7–5 – one-sided as it seemed, belied the quality of opposition that Djokovic displayed on that cool day in Paris. Aside from a default at the US Open, where he was disqualified after inadvertently hitting a ball into the throat of a line judge, Djokovic hadn't lost a match the entire year. Granted, owing to the global pandemic, it had been a severely truncated season. All the same, coming into the final, the Serb was in stunning form.

But not stunning enough for Rafa. Dressed in baby-blue shirt and shorts, with a bright-red headband, the Spaniard wrapped up the first set 6–0 in just 45 minutes. In tennis, this is known as a bagel. For a player of Djokovic's stature, it was ignominy. It wasn't that he played badly, however, it was just that Rafa was too damn good. He'd been too damn good for the entire tournament, dropping not a single set all the way to ultimate victory.

With just a thousand paying spectators in the Court Philippe Chatrier, all wearing protective face masks, the match had a certain melancholic feel. Rain had necessitated the closure of the stadium's new retractable roof – the first time the French Open final had been played under cover in its entire 130-year history. This amplified the echoes of the balls striking the rackets, and the grunts of both players as they laboured through the rest of the match.

Rafa took the second set with ease, too, his serve placement often pinpoint-perfect. Djokovic, meanwhile, didn't help himself with further unforced errors. Again and again the Serb tried to trip up his opponent with dropshots. Some worked, many didn't. "I wanted to kind of disrupt his rhythm, obviously," he said after the match. "But he was ready. He was there, he was prepared."

OPPOSITE TOP LEFT AND RIGHT: Rafa battles Novak Djokovic beneath the roof of Court Philippe Chatrier at the 2020 French Open.

OPPOSITE BOTTOM: The victory was Rafa's 13th Roland Garros title and his 20th Grand Slam singles title overall.

By the time the third set came round, Djokovic managed to put up more of a fight. After an early break of his serve, he himself broke Rafa's serve – the only time in the entire match – marking the event with a fist-clenched roar.

At five games all, the Serb found himself break point down again. Taking a risk, he struck his serve close to the line. At first it seemed to be in, but subsequently it was called out for a double fault after the chair umpire had examined the mark in the clay.

Psychologically this proved too much for Djokovic. At 6–5 up, Rafa then served out his last game to love, sending his final ace wide to his opponent's back hand, so wide that the Serb could only watch miserably as it passed him by. Then, unusually for a triumph celebration, Rafa sank to his knees instead of falling on his back. With a gaping smile, he pointed his fingers and pumped his arms before jumping back up to sympathise with his opponent. Returning to the middle of the court, he clutched his shirt in both hands and bit it between his teeth, as if he couldn't quite believe victory was his. This was his 100th match at Roland Garros. What a way to win it.

With so few spectators, the trophy ceremony was strangely subdued. By now Rafa and Djokovic had covered their faces with masks so that, for once, Rafa couldn't bite his trophy straight away, though once at the end of the presentation runway, he could, and did.

"Today you showed why you are king of the clay," the vanquished told the victor, with all the respect due to him.

LEFT: Djokovic was gracious in defeat. "Today you showed why you are king of the clay," he said.

OPPOSITE: Hugging the Coupe des Mousquetaires (The Musketeers' Cup).

Rafa himself said: "A win here means everything for me. I have spent most of the most important moments in my career here. Just to play here is a true inspiration, and the love story I have with this city and this court is unforgettable."

BBC commentator David Law was awestruck by the significance of Rafa's 20th Grand Slam. "I didn't know whether he had that sort of level of tennis in him at the age of 34," he said. "It is 15 years since he first won this thing. Here he is, in his 30s, playing utterly devastating tennis. Novak Djokovic was made to lose. I don't think two players could have stopped Rafael Nadal today. It is an absolutely massive moment in the sport that he has drawn level with Roger Federer."

The tournament director at Roland Garros was Guy Forget. "It's just beyond anything that anyone could have imagined," he said of the match "Maybe in the future someone will witness something better but, in my mind, that's the biggest sporting achievement any sport will ever see."

"The number of wins that he has made at Roland Garros is incredible. Each time you step on the court with him, you know that you have to climb Mount Everest to win against this guy here."

Novak Djokovic

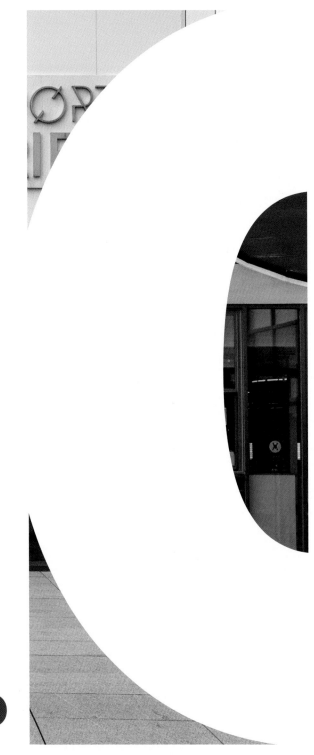

WHAT LIES AHEAD

You know you're famous when astronomers name an asteroid after you. In 2003 the Astronomical Observatory of Mallorca discovered a previously unknown four-km-diameter asteroid zipping round our solar system. Initially they gave it a number designation of 128036. Five years later, after Rafa won his first Wimbledon title, they put in an official request to the International Astronomical Union, asking if they might rename it in honour of their island's most famous son.

And so now, this huge rock careering round our solar system at a speed of 20km a second is known as the Rafael Nadal asteroid.

A more conventional tribute to this great champion can be found at Stade Roland Garros, in Paris, the site of so many of his greatest victories. In May 2021, with the player himself in attendance, a huge statue of Rafa was unveiled, next to the complex's new general public entrance gate, near the Jardin des Mousquetaires. Standing three metres tall, and constructed of stainless steel, the statue captures the Mallorcan as he follows through on one of his mighty forehands.

It's the work of Spanish sculptor Jordi Díez Fernandez, who was alongside Rafa as his creation was unveiled. "What I want to express with the sculpture is a synthesis of all his attributes which can perhaps be boiled down to just one: strength," Fernandez explained. "What I've done is create a sculpture of Rafa Nadal that projects his strength. In actual fact, it's a monument to human strength."

RIGHT: His first Wimbledon victory in 2008.

The first time he met Rafa, the sculptor remembers being astounded by the player's physical presence. "He has the proportions of an extreme athlete. But the fact is he's very down-to-earth, very humble, very approachable, right from the off. If you ask me, Rafa Nadal is an icon, an inspiration to all of us. When we watch Rafa play, he demonstrates all these qualities that, in some way, inspire us to explore the potential within us."

Leading the statue ceremony was the president of the French tennis federation, Gilles Moretton. "Rafa, since 2005, you are a player whose name has been

ABOVE: The statue of Rafa at Roland Garros.

attached to that of Roland Garros," he said in tribute to the 13-time French Open champion. "You've written and you continue to write wonderful history both for the tournament and for yourself."

In a sport such as tennis, which traces its roots back to the 1870s, history is a much revered concept. As in many other well-established sports, tennis fans and players often become slightly obsessed with historical playing records. And there's one record which is far and away considered the most important: the total number of Grand Slam singles titles.

As this book was being prepared, Rafa led this record, with 21 Grand Slams – one more than his two great rivals Roger Federer and Novak Djokovic. Rafa had two Australian Opens, 13 French Opens, two Wimbledons and four US Opens. Djokovic meanwhile had nine Australian Opens, two French Opens, six Wimbledons and three US Opens. Federer had six Australian Opens, one French Open, eight Wimbledons and five US Opens.

We ought to feel privileged to be living in such a golden age of tennis achievement. At no other period in the sport's history have three male players built up such a competitive, exciting and intriguing rivalry. In the entire history of the sport, only five other men (Pete Sampras, Roy Emerson, Bjorn Borg, Rod Laver and Bill Tilden) have won ten or more Grand Slam titles. (In the women's game, by contrast, there are three players who have surpassed 20 Grand Slam singles titles: Steffi Graf with 22, Serena Williams with 23 and Margaret Court with 24.)

Most players attempt to minimise the importance of notching up multiple Grand Slam victories. It's a psychological tactic they employ in order not to feel weighed down by the pressure of all this history, and an effort to focus on the present, rather than worrying about future matches. But the truth is, for the greatest players, it's a goal they always have at the back of their minds; sometimes at the front of their minds.

For American sports journalists, in particular, tennis's Grand Slam tally has become an obsession. It chimes with the wider concept they call "greatest of all time", or GOAT. Pundits, expert and amateur alike, debate endlessly who the GOAT is in each sport, and what results qualify them for that status. In tennis, however, debate is pointless since GOAT status is so clearly defined by the number of Grand Slam singles titles.

Rafa remains rather opaque on the subject. In a 2021 interview in Spanish newspaper *El Pais*, he said: "I have never hidden the fact that I would like to retire as the best in history, and as the player with the most Grand Slams. But I'm not

THE COURTS OF THE KING

There's the Grand Slam, the Golden Slam (all four GS titles plus Olympic Gold) and then there's the Clay Slam – the French Open together with ATP Masters tournaments at Monte Carlo, Rome and Madrid. Only Rafa has a Clay Slam… plus a few Barcelona Open titles.

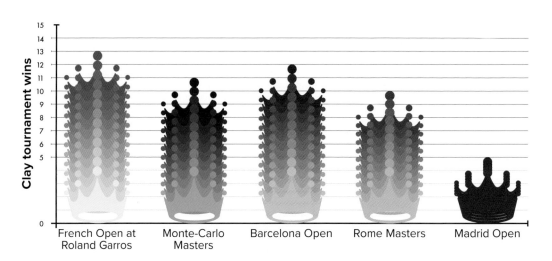

OPPOSITE: After his 10th Roland Garros win in 2017.

RIGHT: At the 2019 ATP Finals in London. From left to right: Dominic Thiem, Novak Djokovic, Matteo Berrettini, Roger Federer, Rafa, Alexander Zverev, Daniil Medvedev and Stefanos Tsitsipas.

going to lose sleep over it. It's not that I don't want to put pressure on myself. I say what I feel: I would love to end my career this way. Of course, it's a goal for me, but I'm not obsessed with it. My principal goal is to be happy with what I do."

Then, after he won his 21st Grand Slam at the Australian Open in January 2022, (thereby overtaking Federer and Djokovic at 20 titles apiece), he said the following: "At the end, it doesn't matter much if one is 21, the other is 20. Or one finishes with 23 or 21. We did very important things for our sport and we achieved our dreams and we enjoy it. I feel lucky to be part of this era that has been very special for our sport."

Rafa and Djokovic are still only in their mid-30s. Provided their bodies hold out, they could both play for another five years, perhaps. Just look at Federer, who is now in his fifth decade. Although the Swiss champion won't admit as much, surely there's only one goal keeping him on court, and that's an attempt to notch up more Grand Slam titles than his two rivals. If you could examine the souls of all three players, perhaps that's what truly motivates them all to the greatest degree.

What does the future hold for this trio? Federer will surely have to retire soon, simply by dint of his ageing body. Djokovic looks to have plenty of fire still in his belly and, on paper at least, has the strongest chance of increasing his Grand Slam tally – although his attitude to Covid vaccines may hamper his ambition somewhat. But what about the man we're most interested in? What can we expect from Rafa?

Asked recently when he might retire, he remained understandably coy. "I do not know. Tennis is a game of the mind. It's not mathematical. When the time comes, I'll know."

When that time finally does come, there's plenty to keep the man busy. All the Nadal family business interests, for example. And the Rafa Nadal Tennis Academy. He recently said he would like to dedicate himself to his charitable foundation, the Rafa Nadal Foundation, which helps underprivileged children.

What about children of his own? While there's no risk of any future little Nadals being underprivileged, Rafa has always insisted he would wait until he had retired from professional tennis before starting a family with his wife Mery. But she is approaching her mid-30s. If he carries on playing for several more years, there's a possibility that tennis and fatherhood may overlap.

"I am a very family-oriented person," he said in an interview in the Argentinean newspaper *La Nacion*. "You never know what will happen in the future, but I

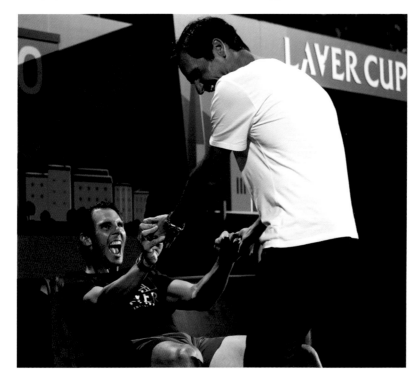

LEFT: With Roger Federer at the Laver Cup in Geneva in 2019.

OPPOSITE: At Roland Garros in 2006.

"In Mallorca, I can be myself. I go to the supermarket and the cinema, and I am just Rafa. Everyone knows me, and it is no big deal. I can go all day – no photographs.

Rafa Nadal

Nadal is the second of three male players in tennis history to have won at least

TWO GRAND SLAM TITLES

each on clay, grass and hard courts. The third is Novak Djokovic, but the first was Sweden's Mats Wilander

He was the first male player to win

CONSECUTIVE GRAND SLAM

tournaments on three different surfaces – clay, grass and hard courts

Rafa shares the record for the most matches won at a single Grand Slam tournament with Roger Federer. They have both

WON 105 MATCHES

– Nadal at the French Open, and Federer at Wimbledon

Nadal is only the third player on the men's tour to win more than

US$100 MILLION

in prize money, along with Novak Djokovic and Roger Federer

Nadal is only the sixth player to be ranked

NO.1

on the ATP tour for more than

200 WEEKS

Nadal has never been taken to five sets in

13 FRENCH OPEN FINALS

at Roland Garros

Between 2005 and 2007 he pulled out an

81-MATCH WINNING STREAK

on clay that started at the Monte-Carlo Masters and ended at the Hamburg Masters. The only person to get remotely close is Guillermo Vilas of Argentina on 53 matches in 1977

Nadal is the first player to win

FOUR GRAND SLAMS

without dropping a set (2008, 2010, 2017 and 2020 French Opens)

John McEnroe believes Rafa's haul of

13 FRENCH OPEN TITLES

will never be beaten

Since turning professional, Rafa has

NEVER LOST

two consecutive matches on clay

Rafa is the **ONLY** male player to win the French Open and the US Open in the same year four times (2010, 2013, 2017, 2019)

Rafa is known for his endurance – he is the No.1 ranked player for pulling out victories from five-set matches, with a winning percentage of

88.2%

In tennis a 'bagel' set is a 6–0 win. Rafa has the

MOST RECORDED BAGELS

against No.1 ranked players.

Nadal has qualified for the season-ending ATP Finals (played between those ranking 1–8 in November) for a record

17 CONSECUTIVE YEARS

(2005–2021)

understand that I will start a family. I will have children. I do not know how many. I love children, but one does not decide unilaterally – that is a matter for two people. I would like to have several children, but I cannot tell you if it's two, or three, or four."

Rafa has explained how he would always measure his success through his personal and family life, rather than by any accumulation of money or tournament titles. "Real success is having friends, having family, taking care of them and feeling loved by people, and the public, which is very important. But it is even more important to feel loved by those who are next to you."

When Rafa thinks of his legacy in tennis, he says he would rather be remembered as a great person than a great tennis player. "In the end, the sport will always be there. What you have achieved will remain. But when [your career] ends, you will be treated for the legacy you have left behind. That legacy is not the titles won, but rather the friends you have left on the circuit; how well you have behaved with the people of the world. And I hope that, during all these years, that is something I have been careful about. I think it is. Wherever I go, people appreciate me – both the tournament organisers and the people on the circuit with whom I hope to stay connected."

During his 21-year career so far, Rafa has achieved so much, it's dazzling. On the court, there have been the 21 Grand Slam singles titles; the further 69 ATP titles; the career Golden Slam; the two Olympic gold medals; the five Davis Cup team victories; the 209 weeks ranked number one in the world; the five times he has finished the year ranked number one; the 81 consecutive wins on clay – the longest single-surface winning streak in Open Era history.

Off the court, we must applaud his academy and charitable foundation. Granted, he was always too busy competing to carry out the hard work in establishing these, but they are grand achievements, nonetheless.

As he looks back on all this, he realises how lucky he has been so far. "I am fortunate in life with everything that has happened to me, with everything I now have. I do things with pleasure and I thank all the people who love me in different places in the world. They are very beautiful things, and I can only thank life."

OPPOSITE TOP LEFT: Playing with kids in Brisbane in 2019.

OPPOSITE TOP RIGHT: Appearing on Spanish TV show *El Hormiguero.*

OPPOSITE BOTTOM LEFT: With ball boys and ball girls after winning the 2017 French Open.

OPPOSITE BOTTOM RIGHT: Nadal returns to Manacor following his victory at the Wimbledon Men's Singles Championship.

THE MATCH

AUSTRALIAN OPEN SINGLES FINAL 2022

January 30th, 2022

Melbourne Park, Melbourne, Australia

Rafa Nadal vs. Daniil Medvedev

Rafa Nadal beat Daniil Medvedev 2–6, 6–7, 6–4, 6–4, 7–5

Was it the greatest comeback of his career? After Rafa clawed his way back from two sets down in the 2022 Australian Open final to win his record 21st Grand Slam singles title, he certainly believed so. So did most of his adoring fans in the Rod Laver Arena.

The effort and physicality he displayed in the heat and humidity of that Melbourne court was impressive enough. But when you consider the flawed lead-up to his Australian Open campaign, then his achievement shines even more brightly.

It wasn't certain the 35-year-old was even going to compete. For most of the previous six months he had been sidelined with a chronic foot injury that had required surgery. This had hampered his training and limited his match practice. At one point he had even feared he might never compete again. Then, just a few weeks before the tournament, the Covid virus struck him down, further disrupting his preparation.

Nonetheless, he arrived in Melbourne as the sixth seed, and in surprisingly spritely form. In the first four rounds, he dropped only one set. Then he was tested: his match against Denis Shapovalov, in the quarter-finals, went to five sets, and his semi-final against Matteo Berrettini to four sets. So, come the final, when his Russian opponent Daniil Medvedev – ten years his junior – surged to a two-sets-to-love lead, fans were sympathetic. It all looked like game over.

But as we've all learned over the years, it's never game over with Rafa. This is arguably the most dogged, unrelenting player ever to step foot on court. Even when he's down in the deepest depths, he's never out.

With Medvedev leading 6–2, 7–6, Rafa needed to draw on all his superpowers to turn the match around. A pivotal moment came in the sixth game of the third set when he found himself facing three break points. He fought off all three.

Then, in the ninth game, the Spaniard saw his chance to strike. Medvedev missed an easy volley, after which Rafa broke serve, and then won the set. It was the foundation he needed to launch his subsequent comeback.

Tension built markedly during the fourth set, which featured a total of 15 break points. Rafa took two of those to set up a deciding fifth set.

Often moving closer to the baseline, in order to pressurise his opponent, he executed some beautifully effective sliced backhands and dropshots. There's no doubt he was also helped by the loudly partisan supporters who, at times, were hawkish in their applauding of Medvedev's unforced errors. The Russian was clearly rattled, even imploring the umpire to rebuke the more unruly among them.

Finally, after a vicious battle that lasted five hours and 24 minutes, Rafa served out the final game to love. He dropped his racket and shook his head in amazement at what he had achieved: a masterstroke; the greatest of great escapes.

"It's just amazing – the way it happened is even more unique," he said afterwards. "This has been one of the most special titles of my career, without a doubt, because coming back after six months without playing and without knowing if my foot can hold a professional match at all, and be able to compete that way, is something unexpected and a big surprise for me."

He described himself as "destroyed physically". Emotions were running high, too. So high, in fact, that he wasn't able to get to sleep after the match that night.

"I feel lucky to achieve one more very special thing in my tennis career," he said after being awarded his 21st Grand Slam trophy. "I don't care much if I am the one or not the one; or the best of the history, or not the best of the history."

But that was just modesty talking. The beaming smile across his face was evidence that this rivalry with Roger Federer and Novak Djokovic to be the overall greatest of all time is a battle he is desperate to win.

The congratulations quickly came in from all quarters. "A final of Herculean proportions," said Australian tennis legend Rod Laver, who awarded the Spaniard his trophy. "Given everything you have endured, this historic victory is so special, Rafa. It has been a privilege to watch you doing what you love."

Former American champion Billie Jean King was equally amazed. "The mental and physical marathon of a five-hour Grand Slam final requires grit, guts, spirit and determination," she said. "What a comeback!"

And Federer was clearly in awe of his rival. "What a match!" he said. "To my friend and great rival, heartfelt congratulations on becoming the first man to win 21 Grand Slam singles titles. Amazing. Never underestimate a great champion. Your incredible work ethic, dedication and fighting spirit are an inspiration to me and countless others around the world."

RAFA AND THE AUTHOR

I'm old enough to have had the privilege of watching Rafa Nadal's entire playing career, from precocious teenager to world-beating 30-something. I've seen the ups. I've seen the downs. I've witnessed the glorious triumphs, and the career-threatening injuries.

The Mallorcan first came to my attention in 2000 when, as a 13-year-old, he won a tournament called Les Petits As in the French town of Tarbes. Considered a junior world championship, this event is a chance for young players to present themselves to the wider world. Sports journalists tend to make a mental note of the winners. Some of those winners find future success in the adult game. Others later fall by the wayside. It was quickly obvious the wayside was nothing that interested young Rafa.

The first time I encountered him in the flesh was in April 2003 at the Monte-Carlo Masters, when he made his debut there. That was the year he famously beat the reigning Roland Garros champion Albert Costa. By that time I was working as editor of a British tennis magazine called *Ace*. A very astute journalist colleague of mine was adamant that this young man from Mallorca had all the makings of a future champion. I wasn't so sure, but I played along anyway, interviewing him for the magazine in the club games room. I remember taking snapshots of him as he leaned down over the pool table, pretending to strike the balls.

It was three and half years later that we met again, with Rafa now growing rapidly into his champion's shoes. It was Paris, in October 2006, and the only time I truly managed to breach the protective wall of PRs and press people that constantly encircle him. *GQ* magazine had commissioned an article from me, and I'd rushed out from London to the French capital on an early-morning Eurostar. The player had been booked to appear on a French sports TV show called *Stade 2*. My chance to interview him was in the courtesy car from his hotel to the TV studios.

Interviews in the back of a car can go either way. If traffic is light and the journey quick, your allotted time might be rudely curtailed. Fortunately, there was severe congestion that day in Paris, and I ended up talking to the man for 45 minutes. Even for a magazine of *GQ*'s stature, that was longer than one would normally expect.

The two of us sat in the back seat of the car, Rafa happy to while away the journey chatting, me trying not to bump up against his colossal shoulders as I pointed my voice recorder in his face. We discussed his love of Mallorca ("I'm sure I'll stay in Mallorca until I'm an old man"), the way he was adapting his playing style so he wouldn't have to run so much on court, and the recent blood doping scandal that his name had been linked to. He brushed off the latter nonchalantly as "complete rubbish".

Then I optimistically broached the subject of his girlfriend, vainly hoping he might reveal some insightful secret. "I don't want to talk about my relations with my girlfriend," he said. "That's my private business. Sometimes they make up stories in the magazines and use private pictures. I don't like this kind of press."

Undeterred, I pressed him on whether Mery (or Xisca, as the media knew her) was a distraction from the serious business of competing at professional tennis. "For me, my girlfriend doesn't help and she doesn't distract," he said. "I have the same results with girlfriend and without girlfriend. I find her one year ago. Before my girlfriend, I win Roland Garros, Rome, Monte Carlo and Barcelona. After girlfriend, I win Madrid, Monte Carlo, Barcelona, Rome and Roland Garros. So it's the same." His body language then made it quite clear this subject was henceforth closed.

Over the years, there were several other chances to speak to Rafa. Most, though, were in the melee of press conferences where it's virtually impossible to glean anything other than rather bland musings on the match just completed. The launch of a video game he was sponsoring in Madrid once gave me another chance for a personal interview, albeit one that was cut short by his communications chief. There was just about time to find out he was a fan of the bands Bon Jovi and U2; that he'd just finished reading novels by Isabel Allende and Dan Brown.

What I was really after was the opportunity to meet Rafa on his home territory. That eventually arrived a few years later, this time thanks to his gym equipment sponsor, who flew me out to Mallorca to interview him for *GQ* magazine, primarily about his fitness regime.

I arrived at his training centre (this was years before he had built his academy) and spent most of the day hanging around, on the promise of an interview. Irritatingly, his communications chief kept moving the goalposts. A morning meeting was pushed back to a lunchtime meeting, which then became an afternoon meeting.

Finally, late in the afternoon, a long drive from the original rendezvous, I was granted an audience. Inevitably, the promised half an hour had been cut back to 20 minutes or so. As ever, though, Rafa was charming. He and I enjoyed an amicable discussion about his gym work, his knee injury, his lasso forehand, Spanish sporting success, his love of gambas a la plancha, the music he played

while working out (Bon Jovi, again). I honestly think he had no idea I had been kept waiting all day, and probably would have been mortified if I'd told him.

All four of my personal encounters with Rafa over the years left me with a similar impression. He is a charming, likeable fellow. Although he is of course immensely wealthy (and deservedly so, given his work ethic), he is not vaguely interested in the VIP trappings of global fame. Nor does he exude that electricity of stardom that many world-famous people do. This may explain why so many describe him as "down-to-earth". He is what the Americans might call a "jock". Sport is pretty much all that interests him, whether that's tennis, football, golf or fishing.

In half a century, when Rafa is an old man, he of course won't be playing tennis or beach football any more. But he'll still be on his Mediterranean island. Don't be surprised if he's still hitting balls on the golf course and fishing off the back of his yacht. Though the yacht will perhaps be larger and more luxurious than his current one.

INDEX

Many thanks to Lorenzo Cazzaniga (tennis journalist and director of *Tennis Magazine Italia* and *Padel Magazine*) for his valuable insights into Rafa's life in Mallorca.

SELECT BIBLIOGRAPHY

- *Rafa: My Story*, by Rafael Nadal and John Carlin (Sphere, 2011)
- *Strokes of Genius: Federer, Nadal, and the Greatest Match Ever Played*, by L. Jon Wertheim (Houghton Mifflin Harcourt, 2009)
- *Roger Federer & Rafael Nadal: The Lives and Careers of Two Tennis Legends*, by Sebastián Fest (Skyhorse, 2018)
- *Bounce: The Myth of Talent and the Power of Practice*, by Matthew Syed (Fourth Estate, 2010)
- *The Best: How Elite Athletes Are Made*, by Mark Williams and Tim Wigmore (Nicholas Brealey, 2020)
- *Lonely Planet Mallorca* (Lonely Planet Global, 2017)
- *The Rough Guide to Mallorca & Menorca* (Rough Guide, 2019)
- *Babolat: An Ongoing Match*, edited by Francois Perrin (Babolat 2011)
- *Dicoculture Illustré de Roland-Garros*, by Julien Pichené and Christophe Thoreau (Editions R&Co, 2013)
- *Rafael Maitre sur Terre*, by Jaume Pujol-Galceran and Manel Serras (Editions Prolongations, 2008)
- *Rafa, Mon Amour: Sa Vie, Son Oeuvre, Sa Legende, Son Mythe*, by Simon Alves, Remi Capber, Pauline Dahlem, Laurent Trupiano, (Editions Flora Consulting, 2013)
- *Rafael Nadal: The Biography*, by Tom Oldfield (John Blake 2009)
- *Right Hand, Left Hand: The multiple award-winning true life scientific detective story*, by Chris McManus (W&N, 2003)
- "'Superstition' in the pigeon," by Burrhus Frederic Skinner (*Journal of Experimental Psychology*, 1948, Vol 38)
- "The advantage of being left-handed in interactive sports", by Norbert Hagemann (*Attention, Perception, & Psychophysics*, 2009)

PICTURE CREDITS